Headhunters

Headhunters

*Matchmaking in the
Labor Market*

**William Finlay
and
James E. Coverdill**

ILR Press
an imprint of
Cornell University Press
Ithaca and London

First published 2002 by Cornell University Press

Printed in the United States of America

Library of Congress Cataloging-in-Publication Data

Finlay, William
   Headhunters: matchmaking in the labor market / William Finlay and James E. Coverdill.
      p. cm.
Includes bibliographical references and index.
      ISBN 0-8014-3927-2
   1. Executives—recruiting. 2. Executives—Selection and appointment.
3. Executive ability. 4. Employees—recruiting. 5. Employees—Selection and appointment. 6. Executive search firms. I. Coverdill, James E. II. Title.
      HF5549.5.R44 F564 2002
      331.12'8—dc21

                                                             2001005661

Cornell University Press strives to use environmentally responsible suppliers and materials to the fullest extent possible in the publishing of its books. Such materials include vegetable-based, low-VOC inks, and acid-free papers that are recycled, totally chlorine-free, or partly composed of nonwood fibers. Books that bear the logo of the FSC (Forest Stewardship Council) use paper taken from forests that have been inspected and certified as meeting the highest standards for environmental and social responsibility. For further information, visit our website at www.cornellpress.cornell.edu.

Cloth printing   10 9 8 7 6 5 4 3 2 1

For Corina and Carlo from William

For my mother and to the memory of my father from Jim

Contents

Acknowledgments

Most fieldworkers depend on the kindness of strangers, and we were no exception. We are deeply indebted to the many headhunters who allowed us to interview them and observe them; their willingness to explain their actions to a couple of academics is what made this book possible. Some respondents went out of their way on more than one occasion to assist our research, and we are most appreciative of their kindness and support.

We wish to thank the Institute for Behavioral Research and the Office of the Vice-President for Research at the University of Georgia for their financial support. This project, like many other qualitative studies, was conducted on the proverbial shoestring, so having access to internal funds made an enormous difference. We are also very grateful to Fran Benson at Cornell University Press for her support and encouragement and to the two reviewers for their many helpful criticisms and suggestions.

Chapter 3 is partly based on our article "The Search Game: Organizational Conflicts and the Use of Headhunters," *Sociological Quarterly* 40(1):11–30 (© 1999 by the Midwest Sociological Society). Chapter 4 is partly based on our article "Risk, Opportunism, and Structural Holes: How Headhunters Manage Clients and Earn Fees," *Work and Occupations* 27(3):377–405 (© 2000 Sage Publications). We are grateful to the University of California Press and Sage Publications, respectively, for permission to use this material.

W. F. AND J. E. C.

Headhunters

1

What Headhunters Do

The Business of Finding People for Jobs

> If you sell, you learn ways of handling emotion, other people's and your own. If you reduce the job to a game or a war, a sale becomes a trick, a score. The idea is to stay in control, to be the puppeteer and not the puppet. The idea is to turn your customer into a friendly opponent.
>
> —David Dorsey, *The Force*

As the United States emerged from recession in the early 1990s, business began to improve at headhunters' offices around the country. Headhunters, also known as executive recruiters and executive search consultants as well as some rather less complimentary names, found that firms not only were eager to hire new employees but were equally willing to contract the task of finding them to third-party intermediaries. Business publications were quick to acknowledge how much headhunters had benefited from the revival of the U.S. economy. For example, an article in *Business Week* in 1994 reported that these were "heady days for headhunters" and that "the executive search business is having its biggest boom since the glory days of economic expansion in the 1970s and early '80s" (April 4, 1994, p. 34). A later issue of the magazine noted that the continued economic expansion of the nineties was keeping headhunters busy (June 2, 1997, p. 26). Even the slowing economy of 2000 and 2001 has not been entirely bad news for headhunters. Corporate layoffs have enlarged the pools of potential job candidates into which headhunters dip and have made employees who have not lost their jobs more willing to take headhunters' calls (*Business Week*, February 13, March 6, and June 25, 2001).

Headhunters are third-party agents who are paid a fee by employers for finding job candidates for them. Their clients are organizations, not job candidates. In some cases a headhunter receives a fee even if none of the candidates he or she produces is hired; more commonly, however, a headhunter earns the fee only if his or her candidate is the one hired. Our book focuses on headhunters of the second type. These headhunters resemble other third-party agents or brokers, such as investment bankers, real estate agents, marriage brokers, and actors' agents, whose fortunes rest on their ability to secure a match between their client and another interested party. Headhunters are the matchmakers of the labor market.

When we started this research we were surprised to find that there had been virtually no scholarly analysis of headhunters. This neglect is odd because there has been considerable academic interest in the processes by which people and jobs are matched—most prominently represented by the work of Mark Granovetter—and there is a voluminous social-scientific literature on the functioning of the labor market. Nevertheless, with the exception of a dated though insightful study by Tomas Martinez (1976), academics have been content to consign headhunters to a residual category of formal matching methods, where they are lumped with advertisements, the U.S. Employment Service, temporary-help agencies, and school placement offices (e.g., Granovetter 1995; Kalleberg et al. 1996; Osterman 1999; Tilly and Tilly 1998). These authors depict formal methods as ineffective and as recruitment techniques of last resort. For example, Granovetter writes that "those who resort to these methods tend to be those who, for more or less structural reasons, lack the right personal contacts" (1995, 20) and that "formal mechanisms that are purely impersonal . . . seem rarely to succeed" (1995, 162). Personal contacts, in comparison, "are of paramount importance in connecting people with jobs" (Granovetter 1995, 22).

We began our project with a sense that this cursory and even dismissive academic portrait of headhunters could not easily be reconciled with anecdotal evidence from other sources. Newspaper and magazine articles, together with the stories we had heard from friends and relatives in the private sector about job offers and job changes following contact (often unsolicited) by headhunters, were incompatible with the last-resort or lack-the-right-contacts argument. Our objective, therefore, was to find out more about headhunters: what they did, how they did it, and why, scholarly indifference notwithstanding, they seemed to be assuming an ever greater role in the matching of employer and employee. We decided to focus our attention on the numerous headhunters based in and around a large and rapidly growing southern metropolis that we call "Southern City."

We found that the headhunters we observed were radically different from the private employment agencies that had existed a generation earlier, as described by Martinez. Until the early 1970s job candidates usually paid the "fee" to the agent, sometimes even if they were not placed with a new employer. It thus cost candidates money, occasionally substantial amounts of money, to get a job through an agency. Some agencies worked out arrangements with employers whereby the hiring company paid the agency's fee as long as the new hire stayed on the job or met other requirements. If the new hire quit, didn't show up, or got fired, then he or she was obliged to bear the cost of the placement fee. In short, job candidates were often forced to accept what might be called a "negative signing bonus"—they had to pay, out of pocket, to get a job through an agency.

Agencies themselves were largely passive when it came to producing pools of candidates. Job hunters approached agencies; an agency's pool of candidates was, in large part, whoever appeared at the door. The function of the employment agent was to persuade some company to hire the candidates the agency had "in stock." What this frequently entailed, as Martinez's book showed so well, was a game of expectations manipulation: a candidate entered the agency with one kind of job in mind, and the agent worked to lower his expectations so that he would be willing to take a lesser job and would, therefore, be easier to place. Candidate-paid fees meant that agents had no compunction about flooding employers with candidates, even if they were not all qualified, because their primary allegiance was to candidates, not employers.

In the past, therefore, the use of an employment agency could well be looked on as a last resort for those without the right personal contacts or social resources. Two major changes transformed the industry during the 1970s, however, and have shaped its current structure. First, payment of fees shifted from candidates to employers. Today the vast majority of private employment agencies—our estimate is that it exceeds 95 percent—charge employers, not the job candidates, the placement fee. Their clients are thus the firms doing the hiring. This fee, and the ensuing client-agency relationship, take two basic forms. Agencies that work on *retainer* are given an exclusive contract to identify and present to the firm candidates for a position. Retained recruiters charge expenses and a fee that customarily is equal to one-third the candidate's expected first-year's compensation. These recruiters typically work on top-level searches—positions paying over $100,000 a year—and include well-known firms such as Korn/Ferry International, SpencerStuart, and Heidrick & Struggles. Agencies that work on *contingency* are paid a fee if and only if they successfully place a candidate with an employer. These agencies are usually in competition with one another to make the placement (although on occasion one will be given an exclusive assignment of short duration), and the fee goes to the one whose candidate is hired. Their fees range from 20 percent to 30 percent of the employee's first-year salary; the typical salary range of positions filled by contingency recruiters is $15,000 to $150,000. These positions consist of mid- and lower-level managerial jobs as well as professional, technical, and office-support jobs (Cole 1985; Lucht 1988). *This book is a study of contingency recruiters.* We estimate that contingency recruiters make up about 85 percent of all recruiters and that they handle over 90 percent of all placements.[1]

The second change is that recruiters today generate candidates for positions. Contingency recruiters in fact devote a considerable portion of their time and resources to identifying, assessing, and stock-piling suitable candidates—hence the term they use to describe themselves: headhunters. Their goal is to penetrate networks that convey information about the characteristics and skills of various people, who are potential job candidates. Recruiters actively seek out and encourage candidates rather than wait for candidates to present themselves to the agency as eager job seekers. Further, they concentrate their search on those who are employed. The difference between traditional employment agencies and headhunters was succinctly summarized by one headhunter: "An employment agency is in the business of finding jobs for people; we're a recruiting firm so we're in the business of finding people for jobs."

---

[1] These estimates are drawn from two industry publications, the *Fordyce Letter*, which is written for contingency recruiters, and *Executive Recruiter News*, which is aimed at retainer recruiters. In reality, the distinction between contingency and retainer recruiters is not as hard and fast as our discussion would suggest. Contingency recruiters on occasion undertake retained searches. A firm is identified as a contingency recruiter if contingency search constitutes its primary source of revenue.

The theory behind headhunters' active identification techniques is very similar to the idea of adverse selection in the insurance field. Candidates who are eager to change jobs (or who are unemployed) are thought to be, on average, less desirable than candidates who are at least reasonably content with their current employment. As in insurance, where the people who need insurance the most are those who are the least desirable from a risk standpoint, those who most want to change jobs are the least attractive as candidates. Star performers, in contrast, are often well treated by their employers and satisfied with their jobs; they neither respond to job advertisements nor contact employment agencies. The only way headhunters can identify and woo such employees is by entering and extracting information from various social networks to learn who the employees are and what it will take to get them to change jobs.

It is hard to be precise about the percentage of positions nationwide that are filled by headhunters. We lack the data that would allow us to compare the percentage of people in professional, technical, managerial, and office-support jobs who acquired their jobs through headhunters with those who acquired them through ads, personal contacts, or online job boards. We have some evidence about the recruitment strategies of employers, however. Data from the National Organizations Survey (NOS) indicate that about 20 percent of all organizations "frequently" use employment agencies to recruit new employees for managerial and administrative positions; 26 percent frequently use employee referrals, and 32 percent frequently use newspaper ads (Kalleberg et al. 1996, 138). These numbers, of course, do not show whether the success rates for the various techniques differ. Moreover, the NOS data are weighted in favor of small firms, which predominate numerically. A 1995 survey of medium-sized firms (one hundred to one thousand employees) conducted by a recruiting-industry newsletter found that 30 percent of these firms "regularly" use headhunters, although it did not provide any percentages for other recruiting techniques (*Fordyce Letter*, December 1995). When one bears in mind that headhunters do virtually no recruiting among new college graduates, these numbers become all the more impressive. Headhunters are a leading, and possibly even the primary, means of recruiting employed candidates who occupy professional and managerial positions.

There is good reason to believe, in addition, that headhunters improve candidates' chances in the labor market. A recent study of

3,062 new hires in a midsized high-technology firm found that the employees who obtained their jobs through a headhunter received higher initial salary offers than those who obtained their jobs in any other way (being referred by a friend, answering an ad, being interviewed on campus, or contacting the company directly). Headhunted hires also received bigger percentage salary increases than those who were hired through any other means, with the exception of those referred by a friend (Seidel, Polzer, and Stewart 2000). Results from a single firm are not conclusive, but in combination with the evidence of headhunters' growing visibility, they support our claim that these agents warrant academic attention.

A Snapshot of Headhunting

All headhunters engage in two basic activities. First, they seek out clients and candidates. Second, they attempt to place candidates with clients. The first activity begins with the job order (JO), or search assignment. This is simply an agreement between a headhunter and an employer that the former will recruit candidates for a position that the latter is seeking to fill and that if one of these candidates is hired, the headhunter will receive a fee. All headhunters, even the most seasoned, have to spend some amount of time generating new JOs, whether it takes the form of rookie recruiters making hundreds of "cold" calls to prospective clients trying, frequently in vain, to drum up some business or veterans checking in with old clients to learn whether they anticipate filling any positions in the near future. Once a headhunter has received and accepted a JO (i.e., she[2] has decided that she has a reasonable prospect of making a placement), she can turn her attention to the task of recruiting qualified candidates. There is no single way of recruiting candidates: a headhunter may find them in her candidate database, through referrals, or through cold calls.

The second activity—placement—occurs after headhunters have identified likely candidates. Placement includes persuading employers to interview and to hire candidates, persuading candidates to go on interviews, "prepping" clients and candidates for these interviews, and if an offer is made, negotiating salary details and helping

---

[2]   We use *he* or *she* interchangeably to refer to headhunters, clients, and candidates instead of the cumbersome *he or she.*

candidates terminate their current employment (which is especially important when a counteroffer is made). Placements are the ultimate determinant of any headhunter's success, for regardless of how good he is at finding clients and candidates, until his clients offer jobs to his candidates and until his candidates accept these offers, he will not earn any fees.

Although the common objectives of all headhunters are search and placement, headhunters employ a variety of techniques and strategies to achieve these goals. The following vignettes, highlighting four Southern City headhunters and the firms they founded, illustrate both the routes they took to become headhunters and some of the different ways in which they go about their work.

George Ferris: Mass Placement in a Local Market

George (firm 5)[3] has been a headhunter for more than twenty years, and he is the owner-manager of one of the biggest firms in our sample. He began his headhunting career in 1980 after working as an accountant, mostly doing internal auditing jobs, for a brief period. He had become bored with this work and decided to join forces with another headhunter. His partner specialized in finding data-processing workers, and George concentrated on finding accountants.

George and his partner split in 1984. The reason, according to George, was that he wanted to expand the business whereas his partner wanted to keep it as a boutique operation. George felt that significant economies of scale could be realized in placing accountants: he wanted to hire additional headhunters and expand the firm's client and customer bases. After starting his own firm, George embarked on his mass-placement strategy. At the time of our interview, over a decade later, he had eleven headhunters in his office, all engaged in placing accountants. In the previous year his firm had placed 295 people, and he estimated that the firm would place around 350 accountants in the current year. He achieves these numbers through a huge database of 15,000 to 16,000 candidates, which, he said, "enables us to move mass, all I can say is mass volumes." He regards this database as his firm's primary asset, although he acknowledges that his headhunters also have to search outside the database if suitable candidates are not located there.

---

[3]   The firm numbers correspond to those in Table 1. All names used here are pseudonyms.

The focus of George's firm's recruiting is middle-management accountants, positions in the range of $30,000 to $70,000 a year. Ninety to 95 percent of his placements are local, which he attributes to the growth of white-collar employment in Southern City in the last decade: "Being in accounting and finance, it's a terrific market we're in, and there's a lot of accountants and finance in the companies here." He does over half his business with four large companies, two of which are headquartered in Southern City. Although one of his competitors dismissed these placements as "cookie cutter" searches, George was unapologetic. Middle management, he said, is where the jobs are, and with his firm's database his headhunters can quickly identify candidates who have the combination of skills specified by the client.

The headhunters George hires all have degrees in accounting or finance. He prefers to hire people with at least five years' experience in accounting because "you need to be able to relate to the people you place," although he agrees that a good headhunter should be capable of recruiting in any industry, regardless of his or her background. He has a firm rule that he will not hire anyone who has worked as a headhunter elsewhere: "I want to train people my own way," he says.

Gail Sanders: Networking in a Local Labor Market

Gail (firm 12) is a solo practitioner who has been a headhunter since 1984. She entered the business after previous careers as a teacher, college admissions representative, and salesperson. Like many headhunters in our sample, particularly those who started in the 1970s and 1980s, she went to an agency seeking a job change and found herself being recruited into headhunting. She finally accepted one of these offers, and in her words, she "absolutely fell in love with it. I knew I'd never do anything else."

Gail welcomed her new firm's emphasis on the consulting and search aspects of headhunting. "I got trained in this business the right way," she says. Instead of being placed in a "bullpen" with a telephone glued to her ear, "dialing for dollars," she was expected to visit the firm's clients. Further, the firm did not advertise for candidates; all candidates were either referred to the firm or recruited directly. The guiding principle was that she was expected to find the best person for the job: "You just don't throw something up against the wall and hope that it's going to stick."

Gail's firm placed clerical workers and secretaries in the local labor market. When the firm began, in the early 1970s, all fees were paid by applicants, but by the time Gail joined it, the shift to client-paid fees had occurred. Gail stayed with the firm after its founder sold it, but she eventually left to join another firm that was adding clerical recruitment to its list of specialties. Her recruiting suffered in the recession of 1990–92, however, and in 1992 she decided to go into business for herself as a solo practitioner, specializing in clerical and secretarial placements. Although hiring was down at this time, Gail was able to increase volume and revenues through a new strategy of charging lower fees for her placements: "I'd rather have 90 percent of the business at 12 to 15 percent instead of, you know, 20 percent of the business at 30 percent." She works at the lower end of the white-collar market: the annual salaries of those she finds and places range from $16,000 to $40,000.

From the outset of her career as a headhunter, Gail has been an enthusiastic networker. Since 1987 she has belonged to a "leads club," a group of female professionals and business associates who meet every Thursday for lunch and to exchange information (or leads) about their respective lines of work. It is an opportunity to acquire new clients and candidates and to elicit the referrals that Gail values so highly: "That kind of personal referral system is a lot better and more effective than advertising, either in the newspaper or any other way, because you've got a personal contact."

Gail is also part of a network of twenty-five solo practitioners who share their job orders and candidates with one another. This network enables her and others to satisfy their clients' demands for speed of service, which is a priority in clerical and secretarial recruitment. A client who wants, say, an executive secretary will not want to be told by Gail that although she doesn't have a suitable candidate in her database, she is certain to find one if she conducts an extensive (and time-consuming) search. The network enables Gail and the other members to tap into one another's databases, thus greatly expanding the pool of qualified candidates they have at their fingertips. In the year before our interview Gail had made sixteen placements that were shared, or "split," with other recruiters.

Frank Brown: Brand Recruiting in the National Market

Frank (firm 20) is the owner-manager of the largest firm in our sample and has been a headhunter for more than thirty years. He entered the business in 1969, following military service as an infantry officer and a brief stint working in the personnel department of a large foundation in New York City. While living in New York, he decided to move back to the South, where he had grown up, to pursue a career as a recruiter. He interviewed at a number of employment agencies in Southern City before accepting a position in a three-person firm.

At the end of his first year on the job Frank approached his employer with a plan for expanding their business. When his employer rejected the idea, Frank started his own recruiting firm, Brown Recruiting, in July 1970. During its first decade and a half the firm was quite indiscriminate in its placements: its focus was junior executives, but it covered a wide range of industries. In the mid-1980s, following a consultant's study of his business, Frank decided to make a major strategic shift. Instead of recruiting across industries, the firm would concentrate its efforts in four main areas, or "disciplines": accounting, sales and marketing, engineering, and junior military officers leaving the services. Every headhunter would work in one of these areas. This was a policy of specialization, or as Frank described it, "brand management." He sees his business as becoming increasingly specialized: "We're very niche-oriented now, much more specialized than even when we started this process." For example, a headhunter in his firm working in the sales and marketing area does not recruit sales and marketing people in general; she instead works a slice of this market, such as pharmaceutical marketing managers.

Growth through specialization has enabled Brown Recruiting to expand to more than one hundred employees, with offices in other cities throughout the country. Its revenues place it in the top 1 percent of recruiting firms nationwide.

Martin Locke: Vertical Specialization in the National Market

Martin (firm 30), another owner-manager, has been a headhunter since 1986. He worked in the retail sector before buying a franchise headhunting firm that specialized in retail placements. When his franchise agreement ended after five years, Martin elected not to renew it, deciding instead to continue headhunting as an independent operator and renaming his firm Retail Search Consultants (RSC).

The firm's focus remains on retail. Martin explained that he had chosen to specialize "vertically," by which he meant that he was "comfortable at placing at any management or executive level" within the retail sector. Like Martin, all the headhunters he hires—at the time of our interview he had four working for him—have retail backgrounds. He feels that the advantage of hiring retailers is that they come with a considerable knowledge of the industry and will be able to learn to headhunt very quickly: "I would say that for them to get to the point where they can make 80 percent of the everyday decisions takes only between three and six months in our business."

The placements that Martin's firm makes cover an enormous range, beginning with $12,000 or $15,000 store-management positions at mall stores such as Regis Salons and continuing upward to senior executive positions at large retailers such as Office Depot or Kmart, where the salaries may be $150,000 or $160,000 a year. The differing levels at which the firm recruits result in widely varying recruitment strategies. At the lowest levels—store managers and the like—the emphasis is on speed: clients expect the headhunter to assemble a qualified pool of candidates quickly, and they expect to make the hiring decision without delay. For these searches, headhunters' efforts are usually quite perfunctory. At the highest levels the emphasis is on quality: clients expect to get candidates who are extremely well qualified for the position, and in order to determine that they have found the best possible candidate, they often take their time over the hiring decision. Headhunters' search efforts here are normally intensive and prolonged. Martin remarked that filling these positions would often take two months or longer: "Where you could put a search to bed in forty-five days before, today we are looking at sixty to seventy-five days on the average, at least we are in our business." Another consequence of the wide spectrum of positions is that there is considerable variation in how much headhunters earn per placement, with fees ranging from $3,000 to $50,000. On the average, Martin said, his headhunters make twelve to fifteen placements in a given year.

The common feature of headhunting at RSC is that it is nationwide. If a client and candidate are local, that is simply coincidental. This means that the headhunters seldom get to see their candidates in person—they have to learn to be effective interviewers and evaluators over the telephone.

A crucial distinction among headhunters is whether they work a national or local market. Headhunters like Frank and Martin, who make placements all around the country, tend to spend a considerable amount of time on search, are unlikely to meet their candidates face to face, and usually have a niche or specialty focus. Variation tends to be across levels of management within a particular sector. Headhunters like George and Gail, who work the local market, are expected by their clients to produce candidates quickly, which means they rely heavily on their databases. They usually meet their candidates in person and tend to specialize in certain occupations with variation across sectors.

Changes in the Labor Market and the Rise of Headhunting

The rise of headhunting reflects two fundamental changes in the U.S. labor market since the 1970s. First, the tie between employer and employee has become weaker. Employers, for example, have become more willing to fire employees as part of corporate reorganizations than they once were; employees, in turn, have been encouraged to think of changing jobs, and even careers, more frequently (Osterman 1999). Headhunters flourish in an environment in which there are lower levels of commitment between employer and employee. Headhunters, we argue, both reflect this environment and promote it: they encourage employees to leave their jobs by telling them that they owe no loyalty to their employers because their employers will not be loyal to them. Second, jobs involving what is called "front-line" or "interactive" customer work—jobs that require a worker to deal directly with a customer—have become increasingly prominent. Frenkel et al. (1999) note that "most new jobs in the near future will tend to be front-line positions in professional and service occupations" (8). Headhunting is one such occupation.

Employer and Employee: The Tie That No Longer Binds
   A central concept in academic analyses of companies and their workforces during the 1960s and 1970s was the "internal labor market." Internal labor markets (ILMs) were depicted as administrative arrangements governing the allocation of jobs and wages to employees within individual firms. They were single-organization career ladders: employees entered the organization at various starting points, depending on their prior skills and education, and progressed upward according to their performance and seniority (Althauser and Kalleberg 1981; Doeringer and Piore 1971).
   Social scientists explained ILMs as implicit bargains between em-

ployers and employees. Employees offered their commitment, loyalty, and hard work to the organization and in return received job security, pay increases, and career advancement (e.g., Thurow 1975;
Stinchcombe 1983; Williamson 1975). Although some critics derided
the faceless conformity of the long-term corporate employee (the
"organization man" in Whyte's [1956] phrase and the "man in the
gray flannel suit" in Wilson's [1955]), the bargain proved enormously
attractive (or seductive) to innumerable white-collar employees. It
rested on the premise that as long as the company avoided serious
economic misfortune, these employees would continue to enjoy
well-paid work and would have little incentive to explore employment opportunities outside the organization.

In the 1990s, however, employers seemingly tore up this bargain as
they began to lay off white-collar employees. The mood of the time
was captured in a series of articles that appeared in the *New York
Times* in 1996 under the heading "The Downsizing of America." The
articles focused on middle-aged white men in middle-management
positions in companies such as Eastman Kodak, AT&T, Sears, and
IBM who found themselves unemployed, many for the first time in
their working lives. During the early 1990s Kodak eliminated 17,000
jobs, AT&T cut 40,000, and Sears and IBM slashed 50,000 and 60,000,
respectively (Ciulla 2000). The *New York Times* reported that at one
company managers were being issued communications guidelines on
how to break the news to employees that they were being laid off.
The newspaper also offered a list of the many euphemisms that had
been coined as alternatives to "firings" and "layoffs": in addition to
"downsizing," there was "decruiting," "de-hiring," "deselected,"
"destaffed," "disemployed," "nonretained," "nonrenewed," "de-
growing," "refocusing of the skill fix," "resource reallocation," "reor-
ganization," "right-sizing," and "work force imbalance correction"
(March 4, 1996).

Layoffs had, of course, occurred on previous occasions, but the job
cutting of the 1990s differed from that of earlier periods in two respects. First, the layoffs were carried out by organizations such as
Kodak, IBM, and Sears that either had no-layoffs policies or had an
implicit commitment to long-term career security (Jacoby 1997,
260–261). Second, although some of the companies that laid off managers were facing increased competition and falling profits, the conventional justifications for corporate cost cutting, many were in good
economic health. Paul Osterman (1999) provides persuasive evidence

of the changing nature of layoffs by comparing the corporate an-
nouncements of job cutting in 1972 with those in 1994. In 1972
nearly 70 percent of the firms announcing layoffs attributed them to
their own poor performance; around 30 percent were due to structural changes that firms made to boost their long-term competitiveness. In 1994 less than half the firms attributed layoffs to poor performance and more than half attributed them to structural adjustments
(Osterman 1999, 39–40). Today's corporation, according to many ob-
servers, is both "lean and mean" (e.g., Harrison 1994).

The impact of these changes can be seen in the declining job
tenure of employees, middle-aged men in particular. (Job tenure refers
to the number of years an employee remains with an employer; the
Bureau of Labor Statistics collects such figures as part of the Current
Population Survey.) In 1983, according to the BLS, the median years
of tenure for men between the ages of 45 and 54 was 12.8; by 2000 it
had dropped to 9.5. Median years of tenure for men aged 55 to 64
dropped from 15.3 to 10.2. In 1983 57.8 percent of men between the
ages of 45 and 49 and 62.3 percent of men between the ages of 50 and
54 had 10 or more years of tenure; in 2000 these numbers had declined to 49.0 and 51.6 percent, respectively (*Monthly Labor Review
Online*, September 2000).

As layoffs have risen and employee job tenure has fallen, the language used to characterize the employment relationship has also
changed. A vice president for human resources at AT&T argued, as
his company was preparing to lay off thousands of workers, that employees needed to abandon old-fashioned notions of job security:
"People need to look at themselves as self-employed, as vendors who
come to this company to sell their skills. In AT&T, we have to promote the whole concept of the workforce being contingent." He
went on to suggest that even the very concept of a "job" was out-
dated and that employees needed to think of their careers in terms of
"projects" and "fields of work," for the society was becoming one
that was "jobless but not workless" (*New York Times*, February 13,
1996). It was statements such as these—and the downsizing that accompanied them—that led management consultants such as Tom
Peters to predict that American workers would increasingly be self-
employed free agents in what has been variously termed an "e-lance
economy" (Malone and Laubacher 1998) and a "free agent nation"
(Pink 1997).

Recent data from the Current Population Survey, however, have cast doubt on the free-agent-nation thesis. Manser and Picot (1999) report that from 1989 to 1997 the number of self-employed Americans *declined* by 246,000, a number that had *increased* by more than 1.6 million in the previous decade. During the 1989–97 period nearly 10.7 million new jobs were created in the United States, with the result that the self-employed share of the U.S. nonagricultural workforce has fallen to under 10 percent (Manser and Picot 1999, 14; see also *New York Times*, December 1, 2000). Downsizing, therefore, has not led to self-employment or at least not on a significant scale, but it does appear to have altered employees' attitudes toward their employers. As part of its series on downsizing, the *New York Times* polled workers about the loyalty of employers to workers and of workers to employers. Seventy-five percent of those surveyed said companies were less loyal to employees than they were ten years earlier; only 6 percent said companies were more loyal. Sixty-four percent said employees were less loyal to their employers than they were ten years earlier; only 9 percent said employees were more loyal (March 4, 1996).

In summary, the U.S. economy since 1990 has been characterized by both enormous job creation and substantial layoffs. Moreover, it is large companies that have been central to both these trends. It was large companies that announced the apparent demise of the organization man and internal labor markets with their job slashing in the early and mid-1990s, and it was in large companies that the growth in employment between 1992 and 2000 occurred: BLS data show that businesses with at least 1,000 employees have grown the fastest since 1994, while the percentage of the workforce employed by companies with fewer than 25 employees has dropped from 30.1 to 29 percent (*New York Times*, December 1, 2000). Even as the economy weakened in 2000 and 2001 and corporate layoffs rose, firms continued to hire. *Business Week* reported in its March 20, 2001, issue that it was "still a seller's job market" for sales and information technology executives; other high-demand areas were marketing, business development, and general management. In August 2001 a *New York Times* article noted that firings "are often going hand in hand with hirings. As companies lose workers in one department, they are adding people with different skills for another . . . continually tailoring their work forces to fit the available work." The article cited a survey of 1,441 companies conducted by the American Management Association which showed that 36 percent of these companies engaged in simultaneous job creation and job elimination in 2000 (August 5, 2001).

The United States has become a high-demand, high-turnover labor market, as companies juggle hirings and firings in order to build a just-in-time workforce and as employees have begun to act on the widespread belief that they cannot count on the loyalty of their employers and should pursue multi-organizational careers. This development has resulted in a recruiting gold rush for headhunters. Employers have turned to headhunters to find workers with the kinds of skills that may not be available within the organization because of downsizing and the disappearance of internal labor markets. Employees, for their part, are willing to listen to headhunters, both to find out what opportunities are available elsewhere and as insurance against future layoffs. The *New York Times* reported that nearly half of managers over age thirty-five speak with headhunters at least quarterly (January 30, 2001).

The Employment Front Line: Interactive Service Work

The overwhelming majority of jobs in the United States today are in the services-providing sector of the economy. The gap between employment in services and employment in the goods-producing sector has been steadily widening since the 1950s; in 1999 there were more than three times as many employees in the former as in the latter (Hatch and Clinton 2000). Many of these jobs require workers to interact directly with customers or clients, to engage in what has been termed "interactive" (Leidner 1993) or "front-line" service work (Frenkel et al. 1999).

Front-line service work ranges from the relatively routine, such as the in-person services provided by waiters and waitresses, retail salesworkers, and hairdressers, to the complex and complicated, such as the brokering activities conducted by management consultants, lawyers, investment bankers, and headhunters (what Robert Reich [1991] refers to as "symbolic-analytic services"). Despite the range of jobs and activities falling under the heading of front-line service work, they have at least two common features. One is that the work involves manipulating the emotions of customers or clients to get them to feel and respond in a certain way. Arlie Russell Hochschild (1983) calls this work "emotional labor." The second is that front-line service jobs of all kinds have been increasing rapidly. Frenkel et al. (1999) have reorganized Census Bureau data on projected occupational growth between 1994 and 2005 into three categories—front-line work, front-line support work, and back-office or manual work—and have found that front-line workers are likely to surpass by far the other two in employment growth between 1994 and 2005. The fastest growing subcategory within the front-line category is that of front-line professionals, who are projected to add three million new jobs in this period (Frenkel et al. 1999, 8).

Despite this growth we know comparatively little about front-line workers and how they manage relations with customers or clients. For example, McCammon and Griffin (2000) state that "the work relationship that is increasingly commonplace in today's work-place—that between workers and their customers, clients, patients, students, passengers, patrons, or prisoners—remains woefully under-studied" (279). Our book is designed to help fill this gap in the literature by showing how headhunters interact with their clients (the companies for which they are recruiting) and with the job candidates they are recruiting for these clients. It is a case study of a front-line service occupation. Headhunting offers a particularly useful vantage point from which to consider the world of the front-line worker because headhunters not only interact with two different sets of customers (clients and candidates) but also mediate between them.

Much of the literature that exists on front-line workers has emphasized their subordination to the combination of managerial and customer demands. Studies such as Hochschild's (1983) and Leidner's (1993) offer a portrait of the front-line worker as someone whose emotions, personalities, and habits of thought have been brought under managerial control in order to satisfy the customer. Part of the explanation for these findings is that they have examined low-level front-line service workers, such as flight attendants and fast-food workers, who are required to handle a large client volume. Frenkel et al. (1999) have shown, however, that high-level front-line workers, such as home loan consultants and computer systems developers, who service relatively few clients, are not subjected to rigorous managerial control; instead, their employers offer them considerable autonomy and expect them to use their initiative to foster long-term relationships with clients. In these cases, Frenkel et al. conclude, "the image of the regimented worker appears to be well off the mark" (1999, 228). Nevertheless, Frenkel et al. claim that customers remain the dominant party in their relationships with front-line workers, even when the latter are skilled and autonomous.

Our argument is a different one. We demonstrate how head-hunters, although they are in a structurally weak position relative to both clients and candidates, manage not just to resist the demands of both kinds of customers but actually to assert some degree of control over them. Headhunters are vulnerable in relation to clients because they are paid on a contingency basis and operate in a highly competitive industry; they are vulnerable in relation to candidates because the latter, with whom they do not have a formal relationship, have to be talked into selling themselves. Headhunters are not nearly as helpless in practice as their structural position might suggest, however. They are quite adept at manipulating and maneuvering relations with clients and candidates in order to control their interactions, thus suggesting that front-line workers may enjoy greater informal power than is often recognized. Our analysis explains how this group of front-line service workers acquires and maintains control over their customers.

Headhunters resist customer demands through a multipronged strategy. One prong is for a headhunter to forge a long-term exclusive relationship with clients, so that clients will use this headhunter alone on search assignments. Another prong is to be selectively disloyal toward clients—to violate, under certain circumstances, the trust that clients have placed in headhunters. A third prong is to use deception to identify likely candidates and then to exploit their insecurities to persuade them to become candidates. A fourth prong is to control the impressions that clients and candidates form of each other before the job interview by supplying them carefully chosen information about each other; the purpose is to ensure that each party enters the interview with a positive impression of the other. A fifth prong is to require that the job offer and acceptance be channeled through the headhunter, to absorb or deflect the anger that each side might otherwise direct at the other, to alleviate their anxieties, and, if necessary, to intimidate candidates into declining counteroffers. Of course, this multipronged control strategy is not always successful. Job interviews go badly despite a headhunter's best impression-management efforts, and counteroffers are accepted despite a headhunter's direst warnings. Nevertheless, the strategy illustrates the range of actions that front-line workers such as headhunters can take to compensate for their relatively weak structural position vis-à-vis their customers.

Data and Methods

The bulk of the research for this study was carried out between 1993 and 1996. Data were collected from contingency headhunters and their clients in a major metropolitan area in the southeastern United States ("Southern City"). Four types of data were gathered. First, we conducted thirty-four semistructured interviews with headhunters, all but one of which were tape-recorded and transcribed. The interviewees were randomly selected by area of specialization from the members' directory of the state association of contingency recruiting firms. The interviewees represented 31 different firms and consisted of 24 white males, 8 white females, and 2 black males. Twenty-eight were owner-managers, 12 of whom were solo practitioners, and 6 headhunters worked as employees of owner-managers. Most head-hunting firms—24 of the 31 in our sample—make placements all around the country. The positions filled by the headhunters include accounting, administrative and office support, banking, data processing, engineering, finance, legal and medical support, insurance, and sales (Table 1).

The interviews were in most cases conducted at the headhunter's place of business and lasted one to three hours. In the interviews we asked headhunters open-ended questions to explore their careers and work, including the development of clients, the production of candidates, and the matching of clients with candidates. In addition, we focused on their decision making, including the criteria they used for deciding whether to undertake a search, how they handled client relations, and how they found candidates. In virtually every interview headhunters spoke at some length, with little or no prompting, about their relationships with clients and candidates.

Second, we carried out more than 300 hours of fieldwork, which took two main forms. We spent approximately 150 hours at five different headhunting firms, observing and talking to headhunters on the job. The firms consisted of one large organization with more than a hundred headhunters, three small companies with three to five headhunters, and one solo practitioner. We had conducted prior interviews with the owner-managers at four of the firms (firms 12, 20, 29, and 30), so the fieldwork enabled us to observe and talk to the other headhunters in these locations. The names we have given to these

Table 1 Headhunter Interviewees

	Number of Headhunters	Specialty Areas	Number of Interviewees	Interviewee Demographics	Name
Firm 1	1	Paper (food engineering)	1	White male	Doug
Firm 2	3	Banking Finance Sales (consumer) Engineering	3	White male White male Black male	Kevin Ben Rich
Firm 3	1	Medical (nurses, office staff)	1	White male	Chuck
Firm 4	6	Accounting Bookkeeping Human resources Legal Office administration Office staffing Office support Secretarial Word processing	1	White female	Sarah
Firm 5	11	Accounting Finance	1	White male	George
Firm 6	1	Engineering (food, pharmaceuticals)	1	White male	Ted
Firm 7	8	Accounting Bookkeeping Finance	1	White male	Stan
Firm 8	1	Sales (investment management)	1	White female	Karen
Firm 9	2	Medical (nurses, office staff)	1	White female	Barbara
Firm 10	4	Food (processing, sales, hospitality, supermarket)	1	White male	Henry
Firm 11	1	Data processing	1	Black male	Dwight
Firm 12	1	Bookkeeping Office administration Office staffing Office support Secretarial Word processing	1	White female	Gail
Firm 13	3	Construction	2	White male White male	Paul Fred
Firm 14	2	Legal (support)	1	White female	Lisa

Table 1 Headhunter Interviewees

	Number of Headhunters	Specialty Areas	Number of Interviewees	Interviewee Demographics	Name
Firm 15	19	Accounting Data processing Engineering Finance Insurance Manufacturing	1	White male	Forrest
Firm 16	4	Engineering Insurance Medical Transportation	1	White male	Scott
Firm 17	1	Accounting Engineering Human resources Management consulting Manufacturing	1	White male	Dan
Firm 18	1	Data processing	1	White male	Jeff
Firm 19	8	Food (retail & restaurant management)	1	White male	Larry
Firm 20	100	Accounting Engineering Sales	1	White male	Frank
Firm 21	1	Accounting Bookkeeping Finance	1	White male	Ray
Firm 22	1	Transportation	1	White male	Dennis
Firm 23	1	Food (manufacturing, sales, marketing)	1	White male	Brian
Firm 24	1	Wireless telecommunications	1	White male	Eric
Firm 25	8	Data processing	1	White male	Dale
Firm 26	7	Engineering Office Staff Sales (corrugated box & paper)	1	White female	Marsha
Firm 27	4	Dental Medical	1	White female	Susan
Firm 28	2	Accounting Human resources Office staffing Office support Secretarial Word processing	1	White female	Michelle

Table 1 Headhunter Interviewees (*continued*)

	Number of Headhunters	Specialty Areas	Number of Interviewees	Interviewee Demographics	Name
Firm 29	3	Accounting Data processing	1	White male	Gene
Firm 30	5	Retail	1	White male	Martin
Firm 31	4	Communications technology Consumer electronics Engineering Product development	1	White male	Randy

firms are Managerial Support Specialists (MSS), Brown Recruiting (BR), Technology Services Associates (TSA), Retail Search Consultants (RSC), and Lincoln Search (LS). Fieldwork provided an opportunity to observe the daily activities of headhunters and to learn how they handled clients and candidates. Much of this involved listening to the headhunter carry on telephone conversations, which he or she would interpret for us once the call ended.

Our second fieldwork site consisted of the various seminars, lectures, luncheons, training sessions, and conferences sponsored by the state and national associations of contingency headhunters. These conferences and other events allowed us to hear well-known speakers (also known as trainers) from the industry address various aspects of headhunting and to talk with the headhunters who were in attendance. Over the four-year span of the project our presence at Southern City events became an opportunity to meet and speak with headhunters we had not yet encountered as well as to follow up with those we had interviewed, observed on the job, or met at one or more previous events. In both fieldwork settings we took extensive notes during the course of the observation or, when that was not possible, as soon as the situation permitted (no later than a couple of hours afterward). The fieldnotes were entered as text documents on our computers within one day of the fieldwork. We wish to emphasize that all names of headhunters and their firms that appear in this book are pseudonyms.

The third kind of data we collected was supplementary, intended to augment and verify the information we had obtained in person. We transcribed and analyzed more than a hundred hours of commercially produced training materials, available on videotapes and audiocassettes, for headhunters. We subscribed to and studied two of the main industry newsletters for recruiters, *Executive Recruiter News* and the *Fordyce Letter*. Finally, we obtained evidence from sixteen employers, either hiring managers or human resources staff, about their use of recruiters. Eleven were randomly selected from the Southern City area; the others were known to us through their contacts with headhunters. This information was also tape-recorded and transcribed.

Fourth, we conducted a mail survey of contingency headhunting firms in the greater Southern City metropolitan area. Between July and October 1995 surveys were mailed to every contingency recruiting firm in the area that we could identify from the state's Association of Personnel Services' Membership Directory, from various telephone directories, and from a sample of recruiting firms generated by a directory-listed sampling frame. A total of 556 firms were thus identified and contacted; 116 surveys were returned to us, including 18 from firms that indicated that they placed temporary employees only or that they mostly did retained searches. Omitting these firms resulted in a final sample of 98 firms, which we estimate to be about one-fifth of all contingency recruiters in the area. Since the response rate was so low, our book makes limited use of these data. Nevertheless, it is instructive to compare this sample with our sample of interviewees. Ninety-five percent of the mail-survey respondents were white compared with 94 percent of the interviewees; 69 percent were male compared with 76 percent of the interviewees; 43 percent were solo practitioners compared with 39 percent of the interviewees. The basic characteristics of the mail-survey respondents and the interviewees thus are quite similar.

Two aspects of our analysis and presentation of the evidence should be noted. First, our analytic strategy was to identify what we saw as the most common and theoretically important ways headhunters viewed issues such as client management, candidate selection, and matchmaking. Second, our presentation of the evidence is couched in terms of observations and interpretations that tend to be typical of the headhunters we interviewed and observed. We do not claim that all headhunters express exactly the same thoughts about how they or their clients behave. We do claim, however, that our portrait captures what is most salient about what headhunters think and do.

2

Theoretical Issues

The Double Sale, the Tertius Gaudens, *and the Visible Hands*

> [A headhunter] needs to be a true broker. A true middleman.
> And the beauty of this business, and that's where my clients
> come in, oftentimes when I've made initial contact with people
> that maybe are at a controller level or a VP of finance, we'll be
> talking for ten or fifteen minutes, and they'll say, "I'm not sure
> why you're calling. Are you looking at me as a candidate or are
> you looking at me as a potential customer?" And I'll say, "I'm
> the middleman. I'm looking at developing a relationship with
> you, and I'm sure something will fall, one side or the other, if
> I'm successful at developing that relationship."
>
> —Ray, A Southern City headhunter

The activities of headhunters shed light on three important issues in
economic and organizational sociology. First, headhunters' matchmaking affords an opportunity to conduct an ethnographic analysis of
an unusual sales process. The labor market is distinct from other
markets in that the products (job candidates) have minds of their own
and come with particular and frequently idiosyncratic interests, preferences, and desires. Consequently, the primary parties to the exchange—employers and job candidates—are actually occupying dual
roles. Employers, who are customarily viewed as buyers, are also selling job opportunities to potential employees. Job seekers, who are
customarily viewed as sellers, are also choosing from the job opportunities and employers offered them. The headhunter's task is to
bring this double sale to completion—to make sure that her client se-
lects one of her candidates and that her candidate accepts her client—

in order to earn her fee. She must prepare both client and candidate to embrace their dual roles of buyer and seller; though each slips into the buyer's role easily, they must often be taught how to sell themselves. We show how headhunters manage the risks of the double sale in order to achieve it.

Second, the example of headhunting highlights the overlooked role of third-party agents or intermediaries in economic transactions. A headhunter is a self-interested third party, what Georg Simmel (1950) called the *tertius gaudens* ("the third who enjoys"), or the third party or intermediary who benefits from managing the unstable and sometimes antagonistic relationship between two others. As third parties, headhunters have the incentive to broker successfully a series of exchanges: between client and candidate, between hiring managers and human resources staff, between the client company and the target company, and between the candidate and his current employer. Despite Simmel's insights into third parties, social scientists have not devoted sufficient attention to understanding how brokers facilitate exchanges that might otherwise break down or erupt into open conflict and how they help define the impressions that people form of one another.

Third, an analysis of headhunting is a way of uncovering the criteria used in screening and hiring new employees. As matchmakers, headhunters play a considerable role in determining how people are selected for jobs. The decisions they make every day about strong and weak candidates are extraordinarily consequential—for the careers of the individual job seekers and for the creation of inequities in the labor market. Headhunters are the visible hands of the labor market: they are the agents who present job opportunities to potential candidates and who present candidates to employers. If we understand how these agents think and work, we can help explain why gender, race, and other ascriptive characteristics continue to be such a prominent feature of organizational life.

The issues just discussed can be posed in the form of three questions: (1) *How are headhunters able to accomplish the double sale?* (2) *What advantages do employers derive from using third-party agents to handle candidate search and recruitment?* and (3) *What criteria do headhunters use in selecting candidates?* These questions provide the theoretical focus of our book.

The Double Sale and the Management of Risk

Various studies of salesworkers have identified the conversion of "prospects" into "customers" as the central goal of these workers (e.g., Benson 1988; Biggart 1989; Leidner 1993; Oakes 1990; Prus 1989a). All saleswork entails persuading a potential buyer to buy the product. This task is, in a sense, twice as difficult for headhunters because they confront not one but two potential buyers or prospects. A brief review of the sequence of hurdles a headhunter must surmount in order to make a placement (and thus earn a fee) indicates just how daunting the entire double-sale process can be.

First, the headhunter must obtain the job order, or search assignment. Sometimes, if the headhunter is fortunate, an employer calls and offers her the assignment; more commonly, headhunters find themselves calling potential clients and former clients seeking JOs. Second, assuming the headhunter has successfully obtained a job order, she must assess her likelihood of filling it. Factors making up the assessment include the number of other headhunters working on the same assignment, how attractive the opportunity is likely to appear to prospective candidates, and whether she thinks she can find candidates who meet the qualifications the client has specified. Third, once she has located qualified individuals, she has to persuade them to become job candidates. Since they are likely to be employees of other organizations and hesitant, for personal or professional reasons, to go on the market, it is not easy to turn them into avid job seekers. Fourth, once she has obtained one or more candidates, she must decide how to present them to the client in the most flattering light. Simultaneously, she must prep the client to put its best foot forward when meeting the candidates during the interviews. Finally, if her client decides to hire one of these candidates, she has to ensure that the content and tone of the offer gratify the candidate's compensation demands and stroke his ego; she must also assist the candidate to resign from his current employer, which largely amounts to doing all she can to prevent the candidate from accepting a counteroffer. In short, the product (the candidate) has to be sold *to* the buyer as well as *on* the buyer; the sale will collapse if the buyer doesn't want the product or the product doesn't want the buyer. How do headhunters cope with the unavoidable uncertainty and risk of contingency search?

According to academic studies of saleswork, sellers of a product are most effective when they assert control of their interactions with prospects. The greater the control the seller exerts over the interaction, the more likely the prospect is to become a customer, regardless of whether the setting is a pre–World War II department store (Benson 1988) or the contemporary life-insurance industry (Leidner 1993; Oakes 1990). One of the reasons life-insurance sales personnel, for example, so readily embrace the scripts they are taught to use on prospective customers is that they believe the scripts help them control and manipulate their prospects. The scripts give them the license to be ruthlessly aggressive in pursuit of new customers.

Headhunting is no exception, except that sellers are attempting to control two sets of customers: clients and candidates. The client has to be persuaded to offer the job order and then to take the candidate. The candidate has to be persuaded to go on the market and then to accept the client. To make matters even more complicated, client and candidate have to be manipulated into selling themselves directly to the other because the headhunter is not even present when they first meet each other—at the job interview. If either the client or the candidate performs poorly during the interview, not even a headhunter with the most polished sales technique is likely to be able to effect the match. Headhunters have responded to these difficulties through a three-pronged control strategy that combines client management, candidate manipulation, and third-party impression management.

The primary objective of headhunters' client management is "clientelization" (Geertz 1978). Headhunters want to establish relatively enduring relationships with clients, that is, to receive multiple job orders from and to make multiple placements with the same clients. From a headhunter's perspective, the ideal, if exceptional, client is one who calls her on a regular basis and offers her exclusive assignments (ones in which there is no competition from any other headhunter). Such a relationship represents the pinnacle of clientelization; its appeal for any headhunter is that the client has willingly placed himself in her hands. Clientelized relationships are found in industries as varied as academic book publishing (Powell 1985), Hollywood filmmaking (Faulkner 1983; Bielby and Bielby 1999), and New York garment manufacturing (Uzzi 1997), to name just a few.

Pure clientelization is, however, difficult to achieve in headhunting, where there is little incentive for clients to offer exclusive search assignments. Contingency recruitment means that the client has to pay only the headhunter who supplies the candidate who is hired, which makes it economically rational for the client to have more than one headhunter involved in the search. In fact, clients are likely to be tempted to behave deceitfully—to offer headhunters apparently exclusive assignments while continuing to entertain candidates submitted by other headhunters. The problem for headhunters is that their structural position vis-à-vis employers is much weaker than that of, say, Hollywood talent agencies vis-à-vis the studios or networks. The leading Hollywood agencies, as Bielby and Bielby (1999) point out, combine their products (directors, producers, writers, and actors) into one unit and market it to studio or network as a single take-it-or-leave-it package. Their power derives from the fact that they control access to and represent the talent on which Hollywood film production depends.

In other agent-client relationships clientelization is achieved through "embeddedness" (Granovetter 1985; Uzzi 1996, 1997, 1999). Embedded economic exchanges between organizations frequently rest on the social or nonbusiness ties between individuals in those organizations. A lending officer in a bank, for example, is more likely to lend money to a client if he knows the person socially (Uzzi 1999). Personal connections—belonging to the same country club or having one's children play on the same Little League team—reduce the danger that either party will behave opportunistically toward the other. An embeddedness argument has also been advanced to explain the business practices of immigrant ethnic groups. Members of such groups lend money to other members, knowing that the strength of group ties is the primary guarantor of repayment (Portes and Sensenbrenner 1993).

Headhunter-client relationships are seldom embedded, however. Most headhunters service clients all around the country, which means they are not going to see many on the golf course or in church. In fact, it is quite common for headhunters never to have seen their clients at all, although some headhunters make a point of meeting their clients. But even in those cases in which headhunter and client have more than a telephone acquaintanceship, getting job orders is rarely attributed to social ties.

In sum, headhunters enjoy neither a structurally advantageous position relative to their clients nor embedded ties with them. The headhunters' version of clientelization is, therefore, undeveloped. To compensate for their weakness, headhunters supplement their clientelization efforts with two auxiliary practices: they subject their clients to close scrutiny, and on occasion they betray these clients. Client scrutiny means that headhunters calibrate the effort they invest in a search according to their assessment of the quality of the job order and client. Client betrayal means that headhunters determine the circumstances under which it is acceptable to violate the unwritten rule that they should not recruit candidates from firms that are clients. Headhunters' management of clients thus has a more adversarial tone to it than is found in other client-provider relationships. There is much less evidence of the trust between the parties that is often regarded as the hallmark of such relationships (e.g., Larson 1992; Lazerson 1988; Powell 1990; Uzzi 1996).

The other group with whom headhunters must deal are candidates. Unlike employers, who are not expected to be hostile to the idea of becoming clients because all employers need new employees at some time (although *this* employer may not want to be a client of *that* headhunter), candidates have to be created. To be more precise, prospects have to be turned into candidates. It is in this sense that the saleswork component of headhunting is most apparent. Headhunters behave very similarly to other salespeople whose goal is to turn prospects into customers (Leidner 1993; Oakes 1990; Prus 1989a): they exploit prospects' weaknesses and fears, and they restrict and manipulate the information presented to prospects. Headhunters, like other salesworkers, are suspicious of prospects who are too eager to become customers—it could mean that the candidate is unhappy with his or her current job, and they prefer to recruit happy employees. Headhunters, again like other salesworkers, believe that controlling their interactions with prospects is the key, first, to turning them from potential to actual candidates and, second, should the job be offered, to closing them on this offer.

As we have noted, headhunters are unlike other salesworkers in that they have two sets of customers and a double sale to manage. Further, the crucial moment of the double sale—the job interview—occurs outside the headhunter's presence. Headhunters rely on the third prong of their control strategy, impression management, to compensate for their absence.

Social scientists have studied how job candidates attempt to manage the impressions that interviewers form of them (e.g., Giacalone and Rosenfeld 1989; Gilmore and Ferris 1989; Rosenfeld, Giacalone, and Riordan 1995). This literature, however, has little to say about the role of third parties in impression management. Third parties and third-party impression management, we argue, are critical to realizing the double sale. Headhunters, in fact, are engaged in impression management almost from the outset, for this is what they are doing when they persuade client and candidate each to enact the dual role of buyer and seller. Their efforts to create a favorable image of the candidate in the mind of the client and an equally favorable one of the client in the mind of the candidate are what we term *direct* impression management. Their efforts to get client and candidate to present themselves during the interview in a light that headhunters know will be pleasing to the other party are what we call *indirect* impression management. Headhunters thus not only pick candidates who they believe possess the characteristics and qualities desired by their clients but also try to make sure that the candidates themselves highlight these characteristics and qualities during their interviews.

The *Tertius Gaudens* and the Externalization of Search

The emergence of headhunting signifies the externalization to the market of a function—the search for and recruitment of new employees—that has traditionally been performed inside the firm. It is an illustration of vertical *dis*integration, akin to the breakup of the studio system and the rise of the independent production company in the Hollywood film industry (Baker and Faulkner 1991a; Christopher and Storper 1989; Faulkner and Anderson 1987) or to the role of independent offshore oil supply companies in European offshore oil production (Hallwood 1990).

There has been considerable discussion of the economics of externalization, much of it stimulated by the "transaction-costs" model. This model seeks to answer a deceptively simple question: When should a firm make a good or service rather than buy it from another firm? The answer is that firms do what is most efficient, that is, they seek to economize on their transaction costs. These costs include how often the buyer purchases the product or service from the seller, the availability to the buyer of substitute exchange partners, and the risk to the buyer that the seller will behave opportunistically (Williamson 1985, 1994). If the transaction is infrequent, if the buyer can get the product or service from other sellers, and if opportunistic bargaining is uncommon, the buyer is likely to buy the product or service.

We argue that transaction-costs reasoning explains, up to a point, why firms use headhunters to find job candidates. It makes sound economic sense for any employer seeking to fill one or two positions with hard-to-find candidates to turn to a headhunter. The latter, as specialists in particular segments of the labor market, know who the best potential candidates are and where to find them. Further, they can achieve economies of scale by servicing multiple clients; a headhunter recognizes that the unsuccessful candidates for a position with one client are where he will begin recruiting when he has a similar search assignment from another client (see Osterman 1999). For an employer, in contrast, it is simply not economically rational to invest time and resources in a search, since he is unlikely to be able to offset the substantial startup costs by spreading them over multiple placements.

A transaction-costs or any other economic theory of hiring is at best a partial explanation for the benefits to employers of using headhunters. Candidate search, recruitment, and, ultimately, hiring are all intensely social processes, in which success rests heavily on relationships maintained, slights avoided, and trust earned. The advantage to using a headhunter, therefore, is not just that he knows how to locate the top candidates quickly; equally important is his knowledge of what it will take to turn a contented employee into a candidate, what might cause the candidate to lose interest in the opportunity, and most crucially, how to get the successful candidate to quit his current job. A successful hiring is, in essence, a deal with many signatories that is brokered by a headhunter. The effective headhunter is a *tertius gaudens* (Simmel 1950), one who can work with all the parties involved. Headhunters' *tertius* strategy has two components to it. Headhunters act partly as a bridge between the parties and partly as a buffer between them.

Consider first the headhunter's bridging role. The main requirement for any headhunter is to connect client and candidate, the essence of headhunting. Headhunters link those who would otherwise remain unconnected. Ronald Burt (1992, 1997) has coined the term *structural holes* to describe these "gaps between nonredundant contacts" (1997, 341); a structural hole presents an entrepreneurial opportunity for a third party to profit from its links to both parties by filling it. Headhunters clearly fill structural holes in the sense described by Burt. Their knowledge of the labor market allows them to connect employers with candidates, thereby generating matches that would otherwise not occur. To assume, however, that headhunters are solely bridges between unconnected parties would be to overlook those occasions on which headhunters are used *even when the client knows exactly who the candidate is he wishes to hire.* This is by no means an everyday occurrence, but it happens. The reason headhunters are used in these "searches" lies in the second component of the *tertius* strategy: the headhunter's role as a buffer.

The buffering role is the opposite of the bridging role. It requires headhunters to come between the various parties that are directly or indirectly involved in the hiring. A potential side effect of a candidate's recruitment and placement is that any one of three difficult relationships—client and candidate, hiring manager and human resources department, and client and source organization—may become inflamed, thereby jeopardizing the hiring. The headhunter's job is to absorb the conflict generated by these relationships to prevent the parties from turning their resentment and even hostility on one another.

The first and, in many respects, most troubled relationship is that between client and candidate. Headhunters often liken the match of client with candidate to a romantic attachment: each side wants to love and be loved with equal strength by the other. As with romantic ties, both parties are exquisitely sensitive to the slightest hint of a loss of interest or enthusiasm by the other. There are two particularly anxious moments for headhunters in this relationship. One is when the client and the candidate meet in the job interview, and the other is when the client extends the job offer to the candidate. Headhunters are almost never present during the job interview, and their influence is thus limited to shaping the impressions that client and candidate form before and during the interview. They exercise far greater influence over the job offer, in terms of both its content and its reception, since most headhunters strongly encourage clients to share the details of the offer with them before extending it to a candidate. If a candidate is happy with the offer, the headhunter has little more to do, but if a candidate is disappointed, she has to try to soothe the latter's bruised feelings. She will press each side to negotiate through her, fearing that the disagreement could easily escalate into a serious rupture if the two parties were to confront each other directly. By carefully regulating the quantity and accuracy of the information she feeds to both sides, she hopes to minimize the discord and create the impression that agreement is within reach.

The second difficult relationship is internal to the client. It is between the person who actually makes the hiring decision (the hiring manager or hiring authority) and the organization's human resources office (HR). Hiring managers use headhunters, in part, as a way of excluding HR from the hiring process. Hiring managers lack the time and knowledge to engage in searches themselves, and they question how effectively the HR staff will conduct searches on their behalf. They feel that HR has its own priorities and cannot be expected to offer unconditional loyalty to any hiring manager. They prefer the unambiguous client-provider relationship they have with headhunters. This is a version of the familiar principal-agent problem: the principal (i.e., the hiring manager) would rather have an agent who is under his direct control and whose goal it is to satisfy him (i.e., a headhunter) than one who is not dependent on him and will assert its own interests (i.e., HR). Headhunters present themselves to hiring managers as agents who will not only be loyal but also help keep HR out of the hiring-decision loop.

The third relationship that headhunters buffer is that between the client and the source organization (i.e., the organization from which the successful candidate is taken). The headhunter's role is to assume responsibility (and take the blame) when a candidate is recruited from a company that is a client's customer or competitor. Overt raiding of a company for its employees is a provocative action that invites retaliation against the offending organization; using a headhunter is a way for the company that is accused of stealing employees to deflect the blame by claiming that it was the headhunter's doing. In many instances, though, that is not true: the client identifies the employee it wants to hire and then employs the headhunter as a cover. The pretense that firms do not recruit candidates from their competitors or customers is a convenient fiction for all parties to accept because it reduces the risk that interfirm tension will erupt into open, tit-for-tat hostility. Headhunters provide a convenient scapegoat if one is needed. Their function is analogous to that of third-party intermediaries in children's "he-said-she-said disputes" (Goodwin 1990). In these arguments one child accuses another of speaking ill of her behind her back, based on a report she has received from a third party. Goodwin points out that the format of the accusations allows a defendant to shift the blame to the third party by claiming that the report is a fabrication. Blaming a third party is a device by which "both accuser and defendant cooperate in maintaining each other's sense of face in the confrontation" (Goodwin 1990, 244). In the case of search, blaming the headhunter allows the client to plead ignorance of the headhunter's activities, thereby limiting the damage to the relationship with the source company.

Visible Hands and Search Criteria

The question of what characteristics employers emphasize in making new hires has generated an enormous academic literature. Part of this literature has focused on the narrower question of whether employers select as employees those who are socially similar to themselves. Social similarity is frequently depicted as a matter of "fit," a concept that has come to assume a central role in the study of employee selection and advancement in modern workplaces. Several influential sociological analyses of corporate life have concluded that managers surround themselves with those who "fit in" and who are the "right sort of person" (e.g., Jackall 1988; Kanter 1993; Moore 1962; Morrill 1995). These studies assert that a candidate's skill plays little part in the selection process once fit has been taken into account. Robert Jackall, for example, states:

> For most managers, however, future chances in an organization, after the crucial break points in a career are reached, are seen to depend not on competence nor on performance as such. Instead, managers see success depending principally on meeting social criteria established by the authority and political alignments—that is, by the fealty and alliance structure—and by the ethos and style of the corporation. (1988, 45)

Managers prefer the socially similar in hiring and promotion decisions, according to Rosabeth Moss Kanter, because it alleviates the uncertainties of trust, communication, and evaluation that pervade corporate life. She argues: "We expect a direct correlation, then, between the degree of uncertainty in a position . . . and a reliance on 'trust' through 'homosocial reproduction'—selection of incumbents on the basis of social similarity" (1993, 54).

We consider the issue of fit vs. skill through our analysis of head-hunters' candidate-selection practices. Although they do not make the final hiring decision, headhunters dictate who makes it into the pool of contenders and thus exert enormous influence over the composition of company workforces. They are, as we have noted, the visible hands of the labor market. We depart from Kanter and others in two ways. First, we argue that skill remains a vital factor in candidate selection. Headhunters, in fact, rely on three factors in evaluating prospective candidates: "specs," "hot buttons," and "chemistry." Specs (short for "specifications") are a general description of the position, the amount of experience and education required of applicants, and the salary. Specs are what one would find in a want ad. They enable a headhunter to identify who should *not* be in the pool of viable candidates, but they do not enable him to discern which candidate or candidates would be really attractive to a client. To distinguish these candidates from the also-rans, headhunters have to pinpoint the two variables that ultimately determine who will be favored: hot buttons and chemistry. Hot buttons are highly specific and even idiosyncratic skills and experiences that a client is often unable to articulate clearly but that she will immediately recognize when she sees them in a candidate. It is through hot buttons rather than specs that skill enters the search and hiring process. Chemistry, which is how head-hunters refer to fit, represents a headhunter's assessment of how well a client and candidate will get along, based on similarities in their backgrounds, interests, and personalities.

Second, we question the connection that Kanter has drawn between uncertainty and fit. She argues that fit is used as a selection criterion only for relatively senior positions where uncertainty is high. Headhunters, however, insist that chemistry is important in every hiring decision: they believe all hirings are based, at least in part, on chemistry. Consequently, headhunters always look for factors conducive to chemistry when they search for candidates for their clients.

The emphasis that headhunters place on chemistry in recruiting candidates has profound implications for candidates' prospects. Headhunters exclude candidates who, for various reasons, are judged to have a less-than-ideal fit with employers. In some cases, naturally, these are candidates who lack the required qualifications or skills. In other cases, however, how well a candidate fits an organization rests on a more subjective assessment: does the candidate have something in common with the client that will generate chemistry between them? Faced with the pressures of place-or-perish contingency search, headhunters have understandably concluded that they are most likely to make the placement if they produce candidates who are socially similar to the hiring manager. Though we do not claim that headhunters recruit socially similar candidates exclusively, they clearly prefer these candidates. Consequently, candidates who receive a low fit evaluation have fewer job opportunities than those who rank above them. This is one explanation why organizational outsiders are excluded from desirable jobs.

In using chemistry to guide their searches, headhunters are inferring client preferences. They believe a client would rather hire someone who is socially similar than someone who is not. At times these preferences include criteria that are discriminatory—most commonly, age and appearance; less commonly, race and gender. The placement imperative means that headhunters reflect rather than resist these preferences. Headhunters, therefore, have a considerable incentive to permit and perpetuate a client's tendency to devalue workers who are older, female, black, or physically unattractive. It should be noted, however, that age and appearance seem to play a more prominent role in headhunters' selection and evaluation of candidates than do either race or gender. Race and gender are among the factors that shape social similarity, but we found little evidence that headhunters' assessments of chemistry were dominated by a candidate's race or gender.

3

Playing the Search Game

The Economics and Politics of Recruitment

It's been our experience that ads tend to yield the best of the unemployed, the best of the unhappy, and the best of the unqualified.

—Steve Finkel, an industry trainer, from his video series "The Art of Recruiting"

A hiring is an expression of mutual attraction between an employer and a job candidate. The hiring manager has selected this candidate, but the candidate has also chosen this manager and organization. Each has sold himself to the other. Job matches occur when hiring managers and candidates concur. From an employer's standpoint, therefore, hiring means identifying the candidate *and* getting her to accept the job.

Organizations have to decide whether the task of recruiting candidates should be performed internally by a personnel or human resources department or should be externalized to a headhunter (or whether to use both internal and external agents). In many instances this decision requires little deliberation. If there is a glut of qualified candidates available in the external labor market and if it is relatively easy to screen them, organizations are likely to do the job internally. Conversely, small organizations without an HR department, such as doctors' offices and restaurants, are likely to favor outside agents, at least for the initial recruitment and screening of candidates. In this chapter we consider the cases that fall somewhere between these two extremes, those cases in which the externalization decision is not automatic. We argue that headhunters are used because they provide economic and political advantages to hiring managers.

An endemic dispute in the sociology of organizations is whether

the decision to perform an activity inside the firm (the "make" decision) rather than outside the firm (the "buy" decision) is motivated
by efficiency or power considerations. On the efficiency side is transaction-costs theory, which asserts that organizations select the make
or buy option depending on which will lower the cost of economic
transactions (Williamson 1985, 1994). On the power side are the various critics of this theory (e.g., Perrow 1986) and others who argue
that organizational actors make this decision to increase their power
over and reduce their dependence on other actors (e.g., Eccles and
White 1988; Fligstein 1985; Pfeffer 1987; Thomas 1994).

Our analysis of the externalization of search suggests that these
perspectives are not always incompatible: organizational decisions do
not have to have *either* an economic *or* a political rationale. The use
of headhunters can be justified on the grounds of efficiency because
they can locate better candidates more quickly than internal agents
can. The economic benefit of using an outside agent lies in the techniques headhunters have devised for finding good candidates, especially those who are happily employed and not necessarily looking to
change jobs. Headhunters, however, also enable hiring managers to
increase their control over the hiring decision. The political benefit
headhunters provide hiring managers is the protection they offer
against two actual or potential threats. The first comes from the
client organization's human resources department, which is perceived as eager to encroach on the hiring manager's right to make independent hiring decisions; headhunters help hiring managers to circumvent the human resources department. The second comes from
other organizations—competitors, clients, and customers—that are
an attractive source of new employees but will resent being raided;
headhunters allow hiring managers to conceal their raiding of their
rivals.

The involvement of headhunters defuses much of the tension that
would otherwise characterize these intra- and interorganizational relationships: conflict is now centered on the headhunter rather than
the hiring manager. Headhunters, therefore, form an insulating layer,
simultaneously protecting hiring managers from their internal chal-
lengers and external competitors and allowing them greater control
over the hiring decision. The art of headhunting—the search game—
is to manage relationships between hiring managers on the one hand
and human resources staff and client/customer companies on the
other so as to maintain the former's authority and independence and

to mitigate the latter's sense of powerlessness, humiliation, and betrayal.

Why Hiring Managers Prefer Headhunters to Human Resources

Headhunters have four key advantages over HR that make them attractive to hiring managers: they search other companies for candidates, they specialize in narrow segments of the labor market, they produce candidates quickly, and they provide such services unhampered by other organizational loyalties or interests.

Search
The conventional view of how people get jobs is that they read help-wanted advertisements in newspapers and then submit their applications. Although many jobs are filled in this fashion, especially those requiring low-level, fairly general skills (Kalleberg et al. 1996), employers frequently seek job candidates whose required mix of skills and experiences are not widely available in the external labor market. Ads are unlikely to be effective in producing the best of these candidates, for as headhunters note, employees who are successful and contented in their current jobs spend far less time scanning the help-wanted ads than those who are not. Ads, in fact, are likely to generate a mixed bag of candidates because candidates must nominate themselves. Some may be quite strong, but many weak candidates will probably also apply. Though the headhunter's maxim that the only people who respond to ads are the unemployed, the unhappy, and the unqualified is something of an overstatement, it highlights the difficulty of producing the top job candidates using this approach to recruitment. George stated bluntly: "The ads type thing do not work, never have in fifteen years." A hiring manager echoed this sentiment: "And usually your really good people in many cases are not looking for a job; therefore, they're not looking in the newspaper ads."

Headhunters reason further that happy employees who are satisfied and productive in their current positions not only ignore ads but actually make the best candidates because a hiring manager is likely to be impressed by a record of success and satisfaction. These are the "hidden" candidates. Scott, a headhunter who specializes in the insurance industry, explained: "There are always those hidden people, and a lot of times they [the hiring managers] want to find those hidden people. They want to find the people that are happy." Finding the hidden candidates in the labor market requires headhunters to conduct candidate searches—to seek candidates rather than wait for them to emerge. Searching for contented and productive employees and then persuading them to become job candidates is what makes headhunters different from newspaper advertisements, as Gail noted: "And that's one of the things that I sell my clients. I tell them . . . the top professionals, they are not looking in the newspaper, because they are happy where they are; and you want somebody who's happy where she is."

For headhunters, effective searching means cultivating networks, monitoring information flows, mining companies for the names of up-and-coming stars, paying attention to the gossip and rumor that characterize all industries, and most important of all, stocking and restocking their pools of actual and potential candidates. The telephone and computer are the tools headhunters use to build their candidate inventories or data banks. They record information, both personal and professional, about the people with whom they have spoken, including age, education, spouse's employment, work experience, job history, and salary history. This information is often highly detailed. For example, a headhunter who recruits brand managers in the beauty products area identifies which accounts her contacts are handling and which products they have launched. Headhunters also seek to pinpoint contacts' "hot buttons," those factors, including desired salary, that would make them willing to change employers. Their purpose is to acquire deep information about companies and candidates in order to learn where to find, say, an experienced commercial loan administrator for a bank; such a search entails knowing how the salary scales and career ladders of other banks in the area compare with the client's as well as what incentives and inducements it will take to pry a potential candidate for this position from her current employer.

It is certainly possible for HR managers to learn the bits and pieces of information just described, but headhunters have the advantage of being able to give their search activities undivided attention. Few if any HR officers can devote the time and effort that headhunters do to cultivating the networks that allow them to discover what will turn a contented employee into a job candidate, which candidate is just looking for a counteroffer and will not accept the job offer, which candidate's family commitments will prevent him from accepting an offer, and who will make an outstanding candidate in three or four years. Well-oiled networks are a highly effective conduit for the rumor, gossip, and other tidbits of information that enable head-hunters to respond swiftly and effectively when an opportunity to find a candidate or make a placement presents itself. Headhunters like George frequently characterize their work as networking:

> Somebody asked me the other day, What is the business about? And I said, I'm going to tell you: I don't care whether you're doing my business or you're doing it on your own trying to find a job, the key is networking. We do the same thing; that's all we do is networking. We ask somebody, Hey, do you know of anybody? They give me two names, I call them, they give me one or two; I mean, it's a networking deal. Well, the difference is we do it every day and we've been doing it for fifteen years and we have the contacts. That's what makes us different than somebody that's doing it once every three years looking for a job and going to church groups or whatever. The networking's the key; that's the way to get a job. . . . We're networking every day; we know what the market's out there; we know what they're having to pay: are you paying enough, are you not paying, are you paying too much, what can I get a four-year person for?

Hiring managers and HR personnel are likely to have too many other responsibilities to be effective networkers. The HR function may well include affirmative-action monitoring, compensation, employee benefits, industrial relations, management development, training, and total-quality-management (TQM) implementation, all reducing the time they have for compiling candidate databases or tracking star performers in other companies. Compounding their difficulties, as HR managers were quick to acknowledge, is that corporate downsizing and other cost-cutting measures have resulted in reductions in the numbers of HR personnel. As one HR manager said, "You've probably heard HR is understaffed; trust me, it's true."

Specialization

Headhunters acquire detailed knowledge through specialization, concentrating their recruiting efforts on narrow segments of the labor market. Frank declared: "We get them all [our recruiters] into these little niches now. If we have a guy placing people in sales, they don't do sales people anymore; they do pharmaceutical marketing managers on a national basis, and they develop a network." Specialization enables a headhunter not only to get to know the members of the pool in which she recruits but to stockpile potential candidates for future searches. A headhunter thus invests her energies in searching for a commercial loan administrator for her present client partly because she knows it is more than likely that at some point in the future another client will also want a commercial loan administrator; only one of her candidates can get the present position, but the others become part of her database for subsequent searches. Brian, a solo practitioner who places plant managers and superintendents in the food industry, extolled the value of specialization:

> For example, if I'm looking for a plant manager for, say, an
> Ocean Spray, I get on the phone and I begin recruiting. And I
> may recruit five, seven, eight candidates for one job, and let's
> say I do fill the job. Well, there are six, seven candidates there
> that I'll put in my database and I'm able to put in my files.
> Okay? The next time I have a job opening for a plant manager
> for, say, somebody like Tropicana, I will have had five, six,
> seven, eight people already in my database that are qualified for
> that, that are in this field.

He went on to say that if an assignment outside his industry was offered to him, he would not accept it because the candidates he generated could not be recycled in future searches (unless, of course, he switched specialties).

The combination of specialization and networking is the key to headhunters' effectiveness; clients can give headhunters a fairly narrow set of job specifications and expect them to produce the right candidates. In contrast, a human resources officer for a food services company conceded that she could not do as well as a headhunter in finding someone with experience to fill a specific position for her organization: "They know where the people are, just because they are so very well connected with the industry, and they're very job specific. If I'm looking for an industrial engineer, they know what companies to go into to find an individual with the skill set we're looking for. Whereas I, myself, may not be that familiar with exactly where to go to seek this person out."

Specialization enables headhunters to achieve economies of scale in recruitment. An HR person, unless he or she is filling multiple and identical positions, is not so fortunate. Instead, HR personnel are far more likely to be filling unrelated positions in different areas, or as George succinctly put it, "one minute they're hiring somebody to empty the trash and the next minute they're hiring an engineer and then they're hiring a controller." One HR vice president at a biopharmaceutical company went so far as to claim that he would not use a pharmaceutical search firm unless it specialized in some aspect of the industry—"they either have a real strong formulations experience, they have regulatory, they have QC management, sales, whatever it might be"—enabling him to match the headhunter's specialty with the position that was open.

Speed

Ad-based hiring is also slow, particularly when it comes to the locating and recruiting of candidates for high-demand technical positions. A company making computer hardware, for example, may have only six months to bring out a new product before its window of opportunity is lost. If it has to hire a team of new personnel to develop this product, it cannot afford to take the time to wait for responses to ads, as Randy, a headhunter specializing in engineering, consumer electronics, and communications technology, pointed out:

> So now they say, Okay, we need a product manager; we're
> going to need three electrical engineers; we're going to need six
> software engineers; we're going to need seven production
> people, production engineers. And all of a sudden they've got to
> have these people within a month's time or two months' period
> of time. There is no way you can advertise with the hope that
> you're going to find the right people in that month and a half.
> The only way you can do it is by recruiting.

Headhunters are motivated and able to fill positions quickly. Motivation comes from the fact that headhunters usually compete with one another to make the placement under winner-takes-all rules. Even if a headhunter is fortunate enough to be given an exclusive search assignment, he has only a short time to produce an acceptable candidate before one or more competing headhunters are notified of the search. Further, headhunters know that an exclusive arrangement does not keep their client from considering unsolicited candidates from competitors who have somehow learned of the search. (We discuss exclusives and competition among headhunters in the next chapter.) A headhunter's success is thus a consequence of producing the best candidates in the shortest time.

By turning to headhunters, employers are, in effect, paying for indirect access to these headhunters' candidate data banks. Such a decision is based on the calculation that the cost of a headhunter's recruitment efforts is compensated by the savings in time, as one employer of data programmers and analysts explained: "We weren't having very much luck finding people using the newspaper, and although a recruiter is a little more of an expense, we were able to find people in a more timely fashion, and get that person in and helping on the projects; I think in the long run it's probably costing us less to use a recruiter."

Many of our interviewees mentioned the speed factor. Kevin, who headhunts for foreign banks' branch offices in the United States, noted: "What people are paying me for is somebody with experience to step in to do something right away and make up for the fact that Joe is now gone." His clients tended to be impatient; if one needed a new underwriter, for instance, he could anticipate a call telling him, "We need somebody to cover our relationship with Georgia Pacific, and he's got to be there two weeks from today." Michelle, who places office staff and office-support personnel, said that if she received a job order on a Monday, her clients expected her to have candidates ready for interviewing on Wednesday or Thursday. By contracting the task of finding candidates to a headhunter, an employer can expect to find three to five qualified candidates (clients usually expect to have at least three candidates) ready to be interviewed in short order and, if the headhunter has done his job properly, eager to accept the job if it is offered. For many employers this is an appealing prospect compared with sorting through what might be hundreds of responses to an ad.

Service

The most important distinction between headhunters and HR is that headhunters must serve their clients effectively or fail. Headhunters are organizational outsiders who earn their fees if and only if a candidate accepts a job he or she is offered. It is on this difference from HR that their attractiveness to hiring managers ultimately rests. Unlike HR, a headhunter has an immediate financial stake in filling a position. Unlike HR, a headhunter can be required to compete with other headhunters in the search for job candidates and can be replaced if the hiring manager is dissatisfied. Unlike HR, a headhunter has one overriding goal: to produce the right candidate for the job and to get the candidate to accept the offer.

Headhunters provide a better service to hiring managers than HR in three respects. First, they are willing to perform the awkward and difficult tasks associated with candidate search, such as making cold calls to potential candidates. In chapter 5 we examine how headhunters persuade satisfied employees to become job candidates; suffice it to note that it frequently represents a formidable challenge to persuade a stranger to don the mantle of an eager job seeker. Employees, especially those content with their jobs, are usually disinclined to put themselves on the market. As Forrest, an owner-manager with more than twenty-five years in the business, put it, "To get on the phone and call people you don't know and ask them to do something they're not interested in doing . . . [takes] nerves, guts, chutzpah, whatever you want to call it, to call people you don't know to try to get them to come to work."

It is often equally difficult to get a candidate to accept a job offer because it requires him or her to exchange the security of a known environment—one in which he or she will probably have performed quite successfully—for the uncertainty of working for a new organization. Headhunters earn their fees when they get their candidates to accept the new job, and hiring managers depend on headhunters to get these candidates into an accepting frame of mind. The headhunter is expected to become so intimately familiar with the candidate's thinking—"almost inside their head," as one employer put it—that he will become a guarantor of the offer's acceptance. Employers would rather not make an offer than undergo the embarrassment and inconvenience of having one declined; the headhunter's job is to make sure that the only outcomes are no offer or an accepted offer. If an offer is declined, one employer said, he would consider that a "big problem" with the headhunter. It is clear that these expectations far exceed those that could be presumed of or imposed on an HR staffer.

Second, headhunters, as outsiders, owe their loyalty solely to the hiring managers for whom they are working. HR, in contrast, has multiple ties within an organization and its own set of priorities that may or may not coincide with what the hiring manager needs. Employee relations, Equal Employment Opportunity (EEO) requirements, and TQM initiatives are among the various responsibilities that companies have assigned to HR. Further, the hiring manager is likely to be competing for HR's time and attention with other managers in the organization. His request for a new commercial loan administrator or industrial engineer who will be able to start in two weeks may very well end up on the back burner if HR's immediate priorities lie elsewhere. By contracting the search to one or more headhunters, however, the hiring authority not only reduces the possibility of friction with HR but gains a partner whose very livelihood depends on satisfying her client by finding a suitable candidate. Headhunters are extraordinarily attentive to hiring authorities' needs and whims because even exclusive arrangements give headhunters no assurance of earning a fee. Hiring authorities have various kinds of leverage over headhunters: they can put headhunters into competition with one another, and they can even employ the ultimate sanction of terminating their relationship with a headhunter.

Headhunters' status as loyal outsiders is also an asset when hiring must be conducted in secrecy. This occurs most commonly when a hiring manager seeks to replace an employee but wishes to keep the firing a secret until a replacement has been hired. (This practice is one way of reducing the inevitable costs that arise from the lag between dismissing one employee and hiring another.) The difficulty, as far as the hiring manager is concerned, is to prevent knowledge of the firing/hiring from reaching the soon-to-be-terminated employee before the hiring manager officially delivers the bad news. When a headhunter is used rather than HR, it is much easier to keep the search confidential. Although pretermination searches of this kind are not typical, they occur often enough to warrant mention. During our interviews two headhunters indicated that they were currently involved in searches in which an incumbent was being replaced.

Third, headhunters do not undermine the organizational stature of hiring managers. A number of organizational studies have attested to the lowly status of HR within the modern corporation (e.g., Jackall 1988; Kanter 1993; Morrill 1995). A practical consequence is that if searches are entrusted to HR, members of this department may end up recruiting, screening, and selecting candidates who earn more than them, an uncomfortable reversal of the normal organizational hierarchy. Forrest explained that organizations were unlikely to boost the status or salary of HR personnel:

> They're not going to pay a staffing person . . . they're not going to have a president making this income, a vice president making this income, a director making this income, a manager making this income, and then a staffing guy making this income. [He used his hand to point out levels of pay, starting off high, going lower, and then going back up very high again for the staffing person.] They're not going to have that.

The advantage of using a headhunter is that neither the amount of money he earns nor his status will threaten the hiring manager's place on the organizational ladder.

As we have seen, hiring managers' preference for headhunters over HR resides in a combination of economic and political factors. A transaction-cost interpretation of the use of headhunters would undoubtedly highlight their role as specialist providers of a scarce resource but would probably overlook their equally important role as hiring managers' loyal allies. Their dual function of finding good candidates quickly and of keeping HR at arm's length accounts for their appeal to hiring managers, who have the power to ensure that they get used. It also means, however, that headhunters represent a clear challenge to both the competence and the jurisdiction of HR, which requires them to figure out how either to mollify or to neutralize HR. The introduction of headhunters, as noted earlier, shifts the conflict over control of hiring from one between hiring managers and HR to one between headhunters and HR.

How Headhunters Negotiate with Human Resources

At one of the firms in which we did our field research a young headhunter had decorated the wall of her cubicle with a poster displaying the now familiar circle with a red slash through it. In the center of the circle were the letters *H.R.* This simple symbol summed up the feelings of many headhunters to whom we spoke about HR. Among the terms headhunters used to describe HR were "roadblock," "speed bump," "obstacle," "quagmire," and "nightmare"; HR personnel were referred to as "weenies" and, in the scathing words of one in-dustry trainer, as people who "didn't have the personality to become morticians." After our interview with him, Kevin sent us a Dilbert cartoon featuring Catbert ("the evil HR director"). Attached to the cartoon was a letter from him stating, "The enclosed cartoon from 'Dilbert' is an eloquent statement of what I was telling you about Human Resources in the American corporate entity. All you have to do is stroke them and they will go away. The problem is the litter box."

To understand headhunters' antipathy toward HR, consider again the triadic relationship created when employee recruitment is con-tracted to headhunters. Although as we have shown, this arrange-ment enhances the autonomy and power of hiring managers at the expense of HR, it does not eliminate HR. Most headhunters find themselves in the position of getting their search assignments from the hiring manager but of having HR as their point of contact with the organization. At a minimum this means that HR will formally notify headhunters that they have been contracted to conduct the search and will sign their checks once searches have been completed successfully; in some cases HR may require the résumés of candi-dates or progress reports during the course of the search. Add to this its role as an organizational gatekeeper that frequently rebuffs head-hunters when they make cold calls seeking search assignments, and it is apparent that HR remains a significant, albeit weakened, player in the contest for influence and status with the capacity to damage a headhunter's prospects of making a placement.

Headhunters belittle HR for a couple of reasons. First, they resent having anyone get between them and the hiring manager. The head-hunters' credo is that good information is the key to making place-ments, and they feel that when they have to go through HR they do not get good information. HR, headhunters argue, is fine for provid-ing general information about job requirements, but they note that when an employer and candidate are successfully matched, it is often due to some subtle points of coincidence between the two, or "chem-istry." Headhunters need direct contact with hiring managers in order to ascertain what the most promising points of coincidence are likely to be. Frank stated: "If we want to place somebody in a high-level marketing position, we want to work with the vice president of marketing in the company. If we're trying to do work in a sales-man-agement function, we want to go to a VP of sales, or if we're doing engineering recruiting and it's in a plant, we want to go to the plant manager. We don't want to go to HR."

Similarly, when a candidate is rejected, usually the decisive factor is not that he or she was unqualified but that the candidate and hiring manager did not quite hit it off or the candidate did not have exactly the right mix of skills and background experience the hiring manager was seeking. It is very difficult to transmit this detailed, nuanced information through HR, or any third party, particularly when HR may possess only a limited grasp of what the job actually involves or why the candidate was unsuitable. George explained, "No HR person, or very few, can tell you exactly what the guy [the hiring manager] wants." In order to make placements, headhunters need information that is both rich and accurate; as an information source, HR is no substitute for the hiring manager, as Ben, who places consumer-sales representatives, emphasized:

> I will work and do work with HR, but I don't want a situation where you [the hiring manager] interview my candidate and I've got to go to HR to hear the feedback on the interview. . . . I want to hear from you why you did or didn't like the person. I don't want to hear from an HR person, "Well, Ben, they didn't like Joe because the experience level wasn't right."
>
> "Well, what part of the experience level wasn't right?"
>
> "Gee, I don't know."

Second, headhunters are well aware that in most organizations HR lacks power and status. They characterize HR as "not really the decision makers" and as the people who are "down at the bottom of any rung in any company because they are not really income producing. . . . I mean, if you've got a basement, that's where HR is." On occasion headhunters even challenge the professionalism of HR, as is evident in the following exchange between a headhunter and a group of HR panelists at a convention. Why was it, the headhunter asked, that "so many HR departments promote a file clerk or secretary to handle recruiting?" At another convention an industry trainer explained what was wrong with HR: the department mostly consisted of young women who leave exactly at quitting time and who spend the last few minutes of the working day "powdering their noses in the bathroom so they'll look nice for their boyfriends in the lobby."

As much as headhunters may look down on HR, it is perilous for them to ignore this department. As we noted earlier, it is standard corporate practice to have HR authorize the use of a headhunter and pay his or her fee. Both headhunters and HR acknowledged that sign ing the checks gave HR a considerable degree of leverage, if only by threatening to withhold payment. Dan, a solo practitioner who places people in a wide range of managerial positions, said: "I don't think you can effectively work around HR. You can get the job done without going through them, but they are the gatekeepers and by and large they sign the check." An HR executive agreed: "Search firm bills are not paid if I don't sign them; it doesn't matter who does the work. So it gives me a little controlling point."

Headhunters thus find themselves in the paradoxical position of having to gain the cooperation of the very people they disparage. Without this cooperation their ability to serve hiring managers effectively is compromised. Headhunters are, therefore, engaged in a very difficult game indeed, for they must avoid antagonizing HR at the same time as they gain and maintain access to hiring managers—and in pursuing the latter goal they are liable to offend HR. Headhunters use three basic strategies to play this game. The first is the high-risk frontal assault, which means overtly and deliberately bypassing HR and going directly to the hiring manager. The second is the covert approach, in which headhunters create the impression that they have bypassed HR by accident. The third is the power strategy, in which headhunters enlist hiring managers as their allies in the effort to circumvent HR.

The frontal assault is generally an act of desperation. Sometimes HR persists in acting as a buffer between the headhunter and a hiring manager even after a search is well under way and candidates have been interviewed. This situation is particularly frustrating for headhunters because they depend so heavily on the feedback from candidate interviews—particularly those in which the candidate was rejected—to guide their search for and preparation of subsequent candidates. Headhunters deem it imperative to learn directly from the hiring manager why the candidate failed. If HR blocks access to the hiring manager, the headhunter may decide that there is nothing to be lost by going over the head of HR and requesting more information from the hiring manager. This kind of brazen disregard for HR's authority will almost certainly cause anger and, on occasion, retaliation. Scott declared: "What we've found is that the HR manager is the one person you don't want to piss off. You don't want to go behind their back because they'll just chop it [the relationship] off as soon as they find out you've done that." An HR manager explained: "That really ticks me off. . . . Because you know they've established a relationship with someone else in the organization, but it kind of leaves you out of the loop. You take your job seriously, and part of your job is recruiting, whether it's directly or indirectly. And so it's kind of like, going through someone else, you lose that control over the job." A ticked-off HR executive is not going to be disposed to cooperate. All headhunters know that they are always faced with actual or potential competition from other headhunters, so they would prefer to keep HR on their side. Although HR may not be able to stop a headhunter directly, it can certainly undermine her efforts. The advantage of a successful covert strategy, in contrast, is that it accomplishes the goal of gaining access to the hiring manager without humiliating HR in the process.

The essence of the covert strategy is getting around HR, either with HR's acquiescence or without its knowledge. An effective way of gaining HR's acquiescence is for the headhunter to ask questions that she knows the HR representative is unable to answer. Karen, who specializes in finding candidates in investment-management sales, explained that she would ask "the more technical-type questions" that she knew would lead to her being referred to the hiring manager. When pressed as to what kinds of questions these were, she responded: "Well, what their goal is, what the target market is, size of the target market that they're working for, what the expectation is first year in terms of a sales goal. . . . Why did the last person fail? What very specific things are you looking for—[questions] they [HR] just really can't answer." Asking hard-to-answer questions is a good device if used occasionally, but it is unlikely to be effective in regular interactions with the same person over any length of time. A variation on this strategy is for the headhunter to call at times when she knows the hiring manager is least likely to have his calls screened, such as before 8 A.M. or after 5:30 P.M., or to call when the HR manager is known to be out of the office.

The following tape-recorded phone conversation provides an excellent example of the covert strategy in practice. Rich, a headhunter who specializes in the construction industry, was making a call purportedly to his HR contact, but what he really wanted was to get some direct feedback from the hiring manager:

Hi, Tammy [the receptionist], this is Rich O. Is Jerry M. [the
HR executive] available? He's left for the day? Oh my God,
we're going to have to dock his pay! What about Chris W. [the
hiring manager]? Is he in? [Tammy transfers the call.] Hey,
Chris how are ya? Good, how's the family? Business good? . . .
Jerry M. had called me in response to a candidate that I faxed
up to him. He's an estimator candidate . . . guy by the name of
Dave K., out of Bacosie. Have you seen that one? Uh huh . . .
Oh, a few weeks ago now . . . Jerry said he was going to call K.
at home that night, but so far he hasn't. And I was just wonder-
ing if there was a serious intent to bring someone in. Umhuh,
umhuh. I see, okay. [Jerry] M. has left already. [After further
discussion of when the résumé was faxed, Rich returns to the
true purpose of the call, which is to figure out what the company really wants in the candidate.] You were looking for
somebody some time ago, weren't you? Estimating. Did you
find him yet? More project engineering/project management
combination, right? You don't need a pure estimator type?
Well, this person, Dave K., has some field involvement also.
[Rich provides some details of Dave's project experience. He
then changes topics and brings up Dave's age, which is a way of
identifying how much experience is required and the likely
salary. Even though it has become apparent to Rich that Dave
does not have the right background, he can use Dave's case to
draw further information from Chris.] This guy is forty to
forty-one years of age, Dave K. is. Umhuh, so what did you say
again, Chris, you need? Umhuh, umhuh. And what are you,
what kind of salary would your guy get? . . . Let me get back to
you with a candidate or two and see what we can do. All right,
thanks, Chris. Goodbye.

After he hung up, Rich explained the rationale for his call and line of
questioning:

> I try to avoid where possible the HR guy because he's depen-
> dent on someone else making the okay. Whereas I go to Chris,
> he can do it, he can make the decision. Now he tells me he
> needs somebody. The way it works. Now I'll remember this.
> This becomes a part of me. This conversation and all of the
> particulars. He is in the small-projects group. . . . So basically

what happens in Chris's group is that he will gct a young project engineer/estimator type and he'll train them. . . . So now if I
come up with a candidate who does what I term bid, buy, and
build—that means they've got to do some estimating . . . then
they have to supervise the building of it—so if I find a young
guy in the five- or six-year experience range, I'll go right back
to Chris and present him. Go right around the weeny, we call
him. HR guy—we call them weenies. We go right around him,
and he can't do anything to me. He might get pissed off and
say, "Hey, I don't want to work with you on this other guy,
Dave K.," that I was working with. But hey, that's no big thing.
He hasn't made any efforts anyway.

Rich believed his relationship with Chris not only would enable him
to get the information he needed in order to conduct effective searches
but also would protect him from HR's discontent at having been bypassed. Enlisting the hiring manager as an ally and protector is the key
to the power approach, the third and most effective strategy for getting around HR. The strategy depends, as we have seen, on the headhunter's having an existing relationship with the hiring manager. If he
does, he can invoke the threat of this manager's intervention to force
HR to cooperate or, better still, the hiring manager can act as the
headhunter's advocate within the organization. The basis of this strategy, as Henry, whose specialties are the food and supermarket industries, noted, is not dismissing HR but "making them know that you're
a power player" and thus gaining HR's respect. Headhunters have all
kinds of ways of letting HR know they're power players. Eric, who
places candidates in wireless telecommunications, told us that a favorite tactic of his was to invite the HR executive to lunch and then to
make sure that the hiring manager was included as well, which would
"cement the two of them together and make sure that this guy [the
HR executive] knows I know him [the hiring manager]."

HR executives acknowledged that notwithstanding their formal
role as organizational gatekeepers, they lacked the authority to op-
pose a hiring manager who wanted to use a particular headhunter. As
one indicated:

You've got some managers that will let you do whatever you
want to do, and they don't care if they've had a ten-year rela-

tionship [with a headhunter] or not. But you've got other managers that are real important in the organization, and they carry
a lot of weight, and they'll come in and say, I want you to use
this agency. And if you have any sense at all, you'll probably
pick up on that hint that you probably should.

Another HR executive said that as far as he was concerned, if a headhunter had a relationship with a hiring manager, then having that
person speak to him "does work for me . . . that opens the door." He
continued: "You have to recognize—I hate to phrase it this way—
who has the power in the organization."

Stealing and Concealing: Headhunters and Interfirm Relations

The second potentially troublesome relationship for hiring managers
is with the other firms—competitors, clients, and customers—that
constitute their organizational environment. The problem here is
that competitors, clients, and customers are better-than-average hiring sources because they are engaged in the same or similar lines of
work. In some cases the hiring manager may even be able to identify
the actual individual(s) he wishes to hire.

A company that hires employees from its vendors or rivals risks a
variety of undesirable consequences. At the very least it will be accused of having a conflict of interest; more likely still will be allegations of unscrupulous business practices, of "dirty pool," as Sarah,
who runs a six-headhunter firm that specializes in office-support
personnel, put it. At worst it could lead to a bidding war between the
companies for each other's employees and possibly even litigation if
the companies have a noncompete agreement (that is, employees
have signed contracts agreeing not to take positions with competitors) or if the targeted company feels that the hiring company is deliberately sabotaging its business.

A firm that uses a headhunter who just happens to recruit from the
firm's competitors, clients, or customers maintains the appearance of
propriety. The involvement of a headhunter turns what may seem to
be an intentional targeting of the employees of neighboring compa-

nies into the accidental result of a disinterested search in the market for the best available job candidates. What is considered "dirty pool" when done by a competing organization is nothing more than competitive forces at work when done by a headhunter. Headhunters thus provide a convenient screen for employers that wish to recruit from firms with which they compete or transact. An employer can finger those individuals it wants to lure away without leaving behind its fingerprints.

Headhunters also provide a good cover for the job candidates who get contacted. An employee who gets a call from the competition asking whether she might be interested in a position may well be reluctant to talk, out of fear that her boss will learn about the contact and conclude that she is "on the market." Talking to a headhunter, however, carries far fewer risks because headhunters call under a variety of guises and for a variety of reasons. Sometimes headhunters call to find out whether someone is interested in becoming a candidate; on other occasions they call simply to gather more information about an industry or other potential candidates. Consequently, employers use headhunters to contact potential candidates, knowing that if a job opportunity is to be proffered, it will be far less obvious than if they, the employers, were doing the calling.

Recruiting from clients and competitors takes different forms. Sometimes a company singles out the individual(s) it wishes to hire and instructs the recruiter to go after this person or persons. George said: "I've had guys come to me and say, 'I can tell you the guy I want, but we can't touch him; he's with a competitor. You recruit him, and we'll pay you a fee. . . . I've had that happen twice recently." Similarly, Scott described his relationship with one of his biggest clients, a reinsurer; this company had an HR department, but the hiring authority still preferred to externalize search: "I've made placements with him by him coming up to me and saying, 'I want you to go contact this person. I know who it is.'" Forrest revealed that he had recently been asked to hire no fewer than fifteen managers from a competitor. In this case the recruiting firm was one of five the employer had hired to raid this competitor in every region of the country in a one-week recruiting blitz.

More common than singling out specific employees, however, is a client's identification of a competitor or customer as a good source of talent in general. For example, Procter and Gamble is often cited by its rivals in the consumer goods sector because of its reputation for developing high-quality managerial talent. Once a specific company is named, the headhunter knows where to begin recruiting, as the following example illustrates:

> For example, you have an account. A client company that says, "We want to get people from Houston's Restaurants. We want managers from Houston's. They work out great. You get those people, we'll hire them." Okay, so we go to our marketing research department and say, "Pull all his lists of all the Houston's Restaurants in the United States," okay. Call those restaurants, ask for the assistant manager or general manager and get that guy or girl. "Hi, I'm with XXX Associates. We're recruiting for a blue chip company; who do you know including yourself that's interested in an opportunity?" It's more definite than that, but that's basically it, the recruiting.

Headhunters are scapegoats as well as screens. If a company is accused of stealing employees, it can point the finger of guilt at its headhunter, as a number of headhunters acknowledged. George said: "Companies have a funny thing about going into another company" because it violates a moral principle of business, "the little unwritten rule about recruiting within each other's organization." But if he did the recruiting, "they can say, 'Oh, this recruiter did it.' See, I'm the bad guy, I'm over here as a scapegoat." Scott said that when one of his clients got him to recruit from one of its vendors, "it lessens the blame for him."

Hiring managers are the primary beneficiaries when the recruitment of new organizational members is contracted to headhunters. Headhunters are simply better at unearthing hard-to-find and even reluctant job candidates than are these managers themselves or their internal agents, their human resources staff. Headhunters provide another major benefit as well: they enhance the power of hiring managers. Hiring managers have a strong incentive to use headhunters on searches that from a strict candidate-availability standpoint might

not warrant it, precisely because headhunters strengthen their organizational position rather than threaten it.

Our finding about the political benefits to hiring managers of using
headhunters is consistent with Eccles and White's (1988) analysis of
inter-profit-center transactions in multidivisional firms. They reported that profit-center managers chose to buy products externally
rather than internally, even when the price of the external goods was
as high or higher than the internal goods, in order to avoid disputes
that might provoke the intervention, and unwelcome scrutiny, of
upper-level managers. An internal transaction over which there was
disagreement about, say, product quality would have to be resolved
internally and could lead to both buyer and seller being blamed by
senior managers; externalizing transactions was thus the buying
managers' way of keeping their superiors at bay.

Our examination of the search game expands on Eccles and
White's and similar "power-process" arguments (Thomas 1994) in
two ways. First, in addition to examining the benefits that third-party
agents such as headhunters provide to organizational members, we
consider the role of these agents in intraorganizational conflicts. Our
analysis suggests that such conflicts become displaced onto the third
party. As we have seen, the focus of tension is the triadic relationship
among HR, the headhunter, and the hiring manager, with most of it
revolving around the headhunter-HR side of the triad. The normal organizational role of HR places it between the hiring manager and the
headhunter, which compels the latter to develop various strategies
for circumventing HR. Although deception is a frequently employed
strategy, headhunters are most effective when they can enlist hiring
managers as allies against HR—in effect using the hiring managers'
authority to enforce the subordination of HR. The nature of headhunters' involvement thus provides further confirmation that organizational outcomes are often a consequence of who wields the most
power.

Second, we show that hiring managers also rely on headhunters to
protect them from challenges from the external environment. The
environmental danger stems from the obvious fact that a firm's customers, clients, and competitors are the best sources for new employee talent. For equally obvious reasons, a company that raids its
clients, customers, or competitors for job candidates invites retaliation, thus jeopardizing its own business interests. By using a head-

hunter, all parties can maintain the pretense that the headhunter just happened upon the right candidate in the customer's or competitor's employment. The smokescreen thrown up by the recruiter thus serves to maintain the sense of trust and propriety on which harmonious interorganizational relationships rest.

4

Managing Risk by Managing Clients

There's no money for a silver-medal contingency recruiter. You either hit the gold or you don't.

—Forrest, A Southern City headhunter

Headhunting can be quite lucrative. An industry survey of contingency headhunters reported that in 1995 the average firm had revenues of nearly $1 million and the average headhunter earned approximately $76,500, an increase of more than 50 percent since 1992, when average earnings were slightly over $50,000 (*Fordyce Letter*, May 1995, March 1996).

Every headhunter's fortunes rest on his ability to secure a match between his client and one of his candidates. Two types of problems lie in the path of a headhunter's success. One is the inherent difficulty of generating candidates and ascertaining whether they are likely to be attractive to clients, issues we discuss at length in chapters 5, 6, and 7. The second is the very real possibility that a headhunter's client will prefer a candidate found by a rival headhunter, in which case the first headhunter's investment of time and resources in the search will have proved fruitless. It is to this second problem that we turn in this chapter.

As already noted, recruiting is an industry with few barriers to entry, and headhunters have no formal means of regulating or restricting the competition among themselves. No matter how good the prior relationship between a client and a headhunter and how high the quality of the service that has been provided, if another headhunter provides a more attractive candidate, there is nothing the first headhunter can do to prevent the second one from offering her candidate to the client and earning the placement fee. A headhunter, therefore, is a risk-taking entrepreneur whose matchmaking efforts are undertaken with the knowledge that failure—resulting from either his inability to find a satisfactory candidate or the production of a better candidate by a competitor—is as likely as success. In fact, failure is more probable than success since employers normally use two or more headhunters on any given search assignment. Compounding these difficulties, the headhunter may not be aware of the extent or even the existence of any competition, for clients have a strong incentive to pretend to each headhunter that he is the only one engaged in the search in order to elicit a maximal effort.

Confronted with an adverse combination of unrestricted competition and potentially opportunistic clients, how do headhunters succeed as entrepreneurs? We argue that they do so through a risk-management strategy in which they consider three factors: how they generated their business (i.e., the assignment to find a job candidate), the quality of the relationship with the client, and the circumstances under which they can justify being disloyal to the client. In short, they manage risk by managing clients.

Headhunters are relatively weak agents because their clients are neither dependent on them nor socially tied to them. The dependence of clients on headhunters is limited by the lack of control that the latter have over the flow of candidates to clients. Headhunters, as we have noted, present candidates but do not represent them. Further, no headhunter is in a position to insist that a client use his services exclusively. The result is that employers are presented with a wide range of candidates, including some from headhunters with whom the employer may have no prior client relationship. Although employers may be circumspect in dealing with headhunters with whom they have not done business in the past, there is no contractual obligation or economic incentive for them to refuse to take a look at candidates generated by an unfamiliar source. Headhunters are, therefore, quite different from Hollywood talent agencies, which represent employees or potential employees and thus control access to the talent. Headhunters also do not have the social ties to their clients arising from membership in a common ethnic community (Portes and Sensenbrenner 1993), from working in the same industry (Uzzi 1997), or from having prior personal relationships (Larson 1992), ties that might be expected to restrain opportunistic client behavior.

Generating Job Orders and Forming Client Relationships

Studies of markets ranging from Moroccan bazaars (Geertz 1978) to academic book publishing (Powell 1985) have found that buyers, when faced with uncertainty about the quality and reliability of goods and services, attempt to form client-like relations with sellers. Geertz refers to this practice as "clientelization," by which he means the tendency "for repetitive purchasers of particular goods and services to establish continuing relationships with particular purveyors of them rather than search widely through the market at each occasion of need" (1978, 30–31). Although headhunters are sellers rather than buyers, they confront an equivalent type of uncertainty and have adopted a similar solution. The uncertainty lies in the fact that it is difficult, first, for headhunters to generate business from new customers (i.e., employers); second, should they receive any such business, they must attempt to determine whether it is worth investing time and energy in trying to make the placement. An unfamiliar customer, like an unfamiliar seller in the bazaar, is a risky proposition. Economic success in headhunting comes from making repeated placements with the same employers—from having clients. Gail observed: "It's a relationship-driven industry, not a placement-driven industry. And those people who don't know how to build those relationships [with clients] are not going to be long-term in this business." To get clients, however, headhunters first need to get job orders.

The lifeblood of headhunting is the search assignment, or job order. It is an agreement between a headhunter and an employer that the headhunter will provide candidates for a position that the employer is seeking to fill and that if one of the headhunter's candidates is hired, the headhunter will receive a fee. Job orders are generated in three main ways: cold calls, in which a headhunter simply calls targeted employers and inquires whether they have any positions that need to be filled; marketing calls, in which a headhunter contacts employers and inquires whether they might be interested in a specific candidate whom the headhunter is promoting; and client calls, in which a headhunter is contacted by an employer and asked if he or she would be willing to undertake a search assignment. Most headhunters use all three methods for generating job orders: we encountered only two headhunters who claimed to make neither cold nor marketing calls.

Few headhunters relish cold-calling. SODing (spinning of the dial) or dialing for dollars, as cold-calling is often described, is distasteful because such a high percentage of calls result in rejection. Nonetheless, nearly all headhunters must do at least a certain amount of calling strangers and asking about job openings; rookie headhunters generally do a great deal of cold-calling (which means that those who make it in the industry have a well-developed tolerance for rejection). The introduction of voice-mail systems has added an additional level of frustration for cold-calling headhunters because it allows targeted hiring managers to screen their calls and to ignore any to which they do not want to respond. Voice mail makes it difficult for headhunters even to speak to hiring managers, let alone get job orders from them.

Headhunters have developed two strategies to mitigate the unpleasantness of cold-calling. The first can be described as targeted cold-calling. A company is contacted when the headhunter has learned from some other source that it is trying to fill a particular opening. The assumption is that the hiring manager will be more likely to accept an unsolicited call if she has a genuine hiring need. A variation on this strategy is calling a company that has opened, say, a branch office in Southern City (information that is readily available from the local business press). The assumption here is that the company will need to do some local hiring and might be more inclined to give this business to a local headhunter.

The second strategy can be described as pre–job order relationship building. The headhunter contacts the potential client merely to "introduce" himself; no job order is solicited. This introduction may be accompanied by a request for a follow-up meeting or the mailing of a brochure describing the headhunter's specialties. The assumption here is that targets will not become clients if they are subjected to a hard sell. Consequently, headhunters must first establish a relationship and build some rapport before they directly request the targeted company's business. It may take months or even years of relationship-building calls to turn the company into a client. Walter, an RSC headhunter, said that he had made eighteen to twenty phone calls to Office Depot over a three-year period before he received his first job order: the company asked him to find a management information systems vice president. He had completed this and subsequent assignments so successfully that in the past year he had earned over $100,000 in billings from Office Depot.

Experienced headhunters prefer marketing calls to pure cold calls because they are less likely to be rebuffed. Marketing calls differ from cold calls in that the headhunter approaches the employer and proffers a job candidate. Ideally, the candidate is someone whose skills are strong and whose qualifications and personality are likely to appeal to the target company. Such a candidate is known as an "MPC"—a most placeable candidate. When headhunters speak of MPCing someone, they mean, in effect, that they are going fishing for a job order with the MPC as bait.

A good marketing call requires a combination of knowing the kinds of candidates likely to impress the employer, having a good candidate, and effectively presenting that candidate's abilities and qualities. Rich outlined his MPC strategy, using the example of an estimator (a person who puts together the cost of windows, bricks, structural steel, and other components of a building's structure) with a design-build, construction-management background:

> I generally ask for the chief estimator. . . . If he happens to be a hiring authority and maybe a principal of the company, I will then start to tell him about a specific candidate that I have. A candidate that I know whose background will fit that particular company. . . . I don't just arbitrarily send this person's résumé to any company. Knowing what this person does, what his strong suit is, I find companies with similar type backgrounds.

Having identified suitable companies, Rich described how he presented an attractive "mental picture" of the candidate to the client:

> The way you present a candidate is very, very critical. I generally start off by, once I get some interest from the hiring authority: "I have a candidate who has a bachelor's in construction engineering from the University of Texas at Lubbock. He has approximately ten years' experience. He got his degree in 1985." This is just the way I'm talking to him. "Most recently, since October of '90, he worked for the Tischman Group, Tischman Construction." And in the industry the hiring au-

thorities are certainly familiar with the large companies, and
certainly Tischman is a large company. And I would go on to
say with Tischman he's an estimator with responsibility for design-build projects. "He's computer literate. Prior to Tischman
he worked for Tailor Woodrow in Tampa, Florida, for approximately four years as a cost engineer. And he is by the way a
professional estimator in the American Society of Professional
Estimators and the American Association of Cost Engineers."
And when I talk about candidates, I keep it from being so
structured—it's like a conversation. I'm imparting information
to them. I'm painting a mental image. I want them to see this
person in their minds and how he or she can fit into a given situation.

In this fashion the headhunter uses the marketing call to highlight
those features of the MPC that he knows will appeal most strongly to
the hiring manager.

There are two advantages to using MPCs to generate job orders.
First, an MPC encourages the prospective client to take the call. The
caller is not approaching empty-handed, as Karen explained:

Just calling and saying, "What openings do you have?"—I
mean, they just don't want to hear from you. But if you go in
there and say, "I'm marketing someone that has ten years' experience, excellent track record selling 401(k) in the middle
market; he's looking to leverage his career," that's much more
effective. I mean, you're going in there with a product that
would be a benefit to them, and that's what you're marketing.

Second, the marketing call lays the foundation for a relationship with
the intended client because, if done effectively, it allows the headhunter to demonstrate that she is familiar with the employer's hiring
needs and has access to candidates who can fill these needs. The
headhunter, in effect, is offering a sample of her wares, with the implicit understanding that more will be available should the employer
become a client.

Headhunters define the ideal client as the employer who calls a
headhunter and offers a job order. An employer may make this call
because he was impressed by a marketing call; because someone else,
either inside or outside the organization, recommended the head-

hunter; or because she was pleased with previous searches undertaken by the headhunter. Whatever the reason, headhunters attach
considerable significance to a client call. They interpret it as proof
that they have established a "relationship" with the client, which
gives them a real shot at making the placement. They believe that
employers are unlikely to have called numerous headhunters—we
examine this point at greater length in the next section—and consequently, that their chances of success are far greater than if they received the job order from a cold call. Headhunters, in turn, work
much harder on job orders they receive from clients' calls than on
those they generate through cold calls, as Gail explained: "If a client
that I have an established relationship with calls me about anything
that they need, that's going to get a priority long before anything I
generated on a cold call."

Only two headhunters told us they made no cold or marketing
calls. Lisa, an owner-manager who places paralegals and legal secretaries in law firms, indicated that she was content to add two to three
new clients a month through referrals, which for her was a painless
way of developing new clients: "Gaining two or three new clients a
month, without any effort, that's enough for me." Henry said he had
so many clients "that it's a full-time job just staying in touch with
these people and [they] are constantly coming back to us for more."
He felt little pressure to generate new clients; he might send letters
to prospects advertising his services, but, he said, "I don't pick up the
phone anymore and call people up and say, 'I just want to tell you
about our company.' Which is sort of nice because I don't like it."
The overwhelming majority of headhunters, however, combine referrals and repeat business with a limited amount of cold or marketing
calls to start new relationships.

The way a job order is generated is of enormous significance because it offers answers to the two intertwined questions that lie at
the heart of contingency headhunting: What is the relationship between employer and headhunter, and what is the likelihood of the
headhunter's making the placement? Veteran headhunters assume
that an employer who gives a job order to a cold-caller has probably
given it to others as well. A headhunter who undertakes a cold
call–generated search will likely be competing with many other
headhunters to make the placement, and the probability of success
will, therefore, be quite small. More commonly still, a targeted employer will respond to a cold call with a rejection, not a job order,

which is an even less auspicious way to begin a relationship with an intended client. Gail claimed, "You can make seventy-five calls and not get one [job order]." Headhunters unequivocally maintain that client calls produce the best job orders, by which they mean job orders most likely to result in placements. Doug, a solo practitioner who places candidates in engineering and management positions in paper mills, stated: "Most anything I've developed in the last few years have been relationships I've developed from years earlier. I'm trying to think—the last placement I did off a cold call, a marketing call, was probably a year and a half ago, maybe two years ago." Nonetheless, not every job order received from a client call is equally likely to result in a placement. Headhunters must evaluate clients and job orders in order to decide how much time, energy, and money to invest in their searches.

Evaluating Assignments and Clients

Headhunters earn their fees when they make placements. Receiving a job order, even a good job order, is merely the first step in a process whose payoff is not realized until a candidate accepts the job offer. Having a job order creates the opportunity for a headhunter; the question is whether he or she can take advantage of it. A number of obstacles confront any headhunter seeking to make a placement, such as a failure to find strong candidates, a client who finds all the candidates unsuitable, candidates who are unwilling to accept the job offer, and better candidates provided by a rival headhunter. Every headhunter has a story or two of searches that were undertaken but should not have been, because of a failure to acknowledge what in retrospect were unmistakable warning signs. Sometimes the excitement of a new job order causes even experienced headhunters to overlook or ignore information about the opening that makes filling it unlikely. The art of contingency headhunting is being able to size up these obstacles accurately before investing efforts and resources in a search—to form, in other words, a reasonably clear picture of the risk-reward trade-off. Headhunters must evaluate both the assignment itself and the client that offered it.

Assignment Evaluation

In evaluating assignments, headhunters pose a fairly standard set of questions to assess their likelihood of making the placement. The first question concerns how long the position has been open. Is it a position that is newly available, or has it been open for some months? If the latter, why has it been open for so long, have any offers been made, and if so, why were they declined? These questions help identify whether there are problems with either the hiring-decision procedures or the job description. Headhunters are particularly leery of organizations in which managers make hiring recommendations to their superiors, who have the final say; headhunters believe the lower-level managers are fearful of recommending someone their boss will reject and so they hesitate to recommend anyone. "They look for reasons to reject candidates," was how Walter put it. Hiring delays may also indicate a lack of agreement about the job description; for example, a high-tech company may need a director of business development, but the managers responsible for making the hire may be unable to agree as to whether candidates should have an engineering or a marketing background.

A second question is why the position is open. If an employee has resigned or has been fired, a headhunter will want to know how long the previous occupant stayed in the position and the circumstances surrounding his or her departure. A headhunter who learns, for example, that this is a position in which no one has lasted more than a year will know to proceed with caution; even if he or she succeeds in making the placement, if the new hire does not last long the headhunter's reputation may be bruised. If the position is open because it has been newly created, there is always a danger of a lack of consensus in the organization about the job description.

A third question concerns the urgency of the hiring decision. As far as headhunters are concerned, the quicker the hiring decision has to be made, the better. Ideally, headhunters seek the proverbial client who needed the position filled yesterday. A lack of urgency, in contrast, means that the hiring decision may be postponed, perhaps indefinitely. To get at this issue headhunters ask for a step-by-step account of the hiring process, paying close attention to the timing of the first and second interviews once candidates have been submitted as well as to the number of managers participating in the hiring decision, which is a good indicator of how rapidly the process will move.

A fourth question concerns the proposed salary for the position. Headhunters need to satisfy themselves that the salary is competitive, that it is accurately set at the current labor-market price for candidates with this particular mix of qualifications, skills, and experience. As Dale, an owner-operator who specialized in the data-processing industry, put it, "If they [the employer] are looking for a five-year person and are looking to pay them [candidates] a two-year salary, then that's ridiculous. I mean, I can't help them." Gail described a recent job order that she had "thrown out" because of an "utterly absurd" starting salary: "They [the client] wanted an entry-level sales person for a Japanese-owned travel agency, and they wanted it to start at $14,400."

A fifth question is whether candidates are available, even at the going rate. All else being equal, a headhunter would rather recruit for a common position in which the supply of candidates is plentiful than for one that requires an unusual background or is extremely specialized. Martin, the owner-manager of RSC, explained what constituted a "hot" job order for him:

> It is not an obscure job, as in quality control and industrial engineering specializing in da, da, da. But instead, in retail, for instance, a buyer of women's tops or bottoms, which is a very common position for a district manager handling eight to twelve women's apparel, fashion apparel stores. These are very typical positions that are out there, as opposed to someone who is in product development of women's earrings.

Larry joked that if candidates for a particular position were extremely scarce, the employer should "call the FBI," not him. "Needle-in-the-haystack" searches, as Eric dubbed them, are rarely a profitable use of the headhunter's time.

A sixth question concerns the fee. Headhunters have to make sure not only that clients are willing to pay a fee but that the fee is commensurate with the difficulty of the search. As might be expected, there is frequently a gap between the fee that headhunters expect to get and the fee that clients are willing to pay. It is quite common for headhunters to anticipate fees of 30 to 35 percent of a new hire's first year's salary but to be offered job orders in which the fees are only 15 to 20 percent. Whether or not a headhunter accepts a low-fee job order depends on his assessment of how difficult it will be to find viable candidates. If the headhunter sees the search as comparatively simple—he knows that good candidates can be located quickly and easily—a 15 percent fee may be acceptable.

We should note that the decision to accept or decline a job order is rarely as uncomplicated as these decision rules might imply. Three factors muddy the waters here. First, a headhunter can directly shape the characteristics of the job order, such as the size of the salary. A headhunter may, for example, inform the client or prospective client that the proposed salary is too low in view of the skills and qualifications that are being sought. If the client accepts this argument, the job order will become more attractive to the headhunter.

Second, there are degrees of acceptance of a job order. The fact that searches are conducted on a contingency basis means that headhunters seldom unequivocally decline a search, even one that fails to satisfy the criteria just described. When headhunters speak of saying no to a job order, what they really mean is that they are not going to engage in a full-scale search for candidates. If they happen to locate a candidate after doing a quick database scan, they will notify the client accordingly (without, however, indicating where they found the candidate or how long it took). Perfunctory searches are a typical response to unsatisfactory job orders, as Eric explained after mentioning that he was still "working on" a job order that was nine months old:

Q: So you're still working on a search from last September?
A: Yep.
Q: That is still open?
A: Yep.
Q: Sounds tough.
A: Well, I'm not working real hard on that. . . . In that particular case, he's trying to hire, it's a BellSouth search, he's trying to hire a new level of person that they've not had in the organization before. They're trying to hire a person who's not just an executive director of sales and marketing but someone who can move into a major city GM [general manager] job within fifteen months. And they want to spend fifteen grand less than the market. And that's why I'm not spending a lot of time on it; I mean, the search is there, and if I run across somebody, great. . . . Now about the only way you're going to find somebody is if you're going to land on somebody who is very unhappy with what they're doing and is willing to take a step back dollar-wise just to get into BellSouth. . . . Can I afford to sit here and pick the phone up and dial it until I find somebody?

A headhunter who has three to eight full-scale searches in progress may have as many as fifteen to twenty other job orders that receive this kind of cursory attention.[1]

Third, on occasion a headhunter believes a job order that appears to be a bad one is actually a good one because of the nature of the relationship he enjoys with his client. A striking demonstration of how job orders can be reinterpreted occurred late one afternoon at RSC. Walter received a call from Office Depot placing a job order for five loss-prevention managers (entry-level managerial positions in the company's stores responsible for store security). By coincidence, earlier that day Walter had referred to his strong relationship with Office Depot, where he has had considerable success in making placements during the past year—with the notable exception of the loss-prevention-manager (LPM) positions, for which all his candidates had been rejected. Walter's explanation of his failure here focused on one of the textbook red flags in headhunting: Office Depot had a "round robin" hiring process in which three regional managers made hiring recommendations to the vice president for operations, who had the final say. This procedure, as any experienced headhunter will confirm, tends to produce a high percentage of reject decisions.

When Walter got the new job order for five LPM positions, however, he elected to disregard both his prior experience and the red flag. In his phone conversation with Rhonda, the human resources manager who placed the order, he had learned that she was under pressure from the operations VP to fill these positions and that there would be no more round robin. He therefore believed it was worth making a serious effort to recruit candidates, thus earning the $8,000 in commission per position. At least that is what he told Martin, the owner-manager, who had walked into his office as he was concluding his conversation with Rhonda. At the mention of her name, Martin screwed up his face in disgust and said, "Rwanda," but Walter continued to argue that this time it would be different. Martin did not respond, but his face made it evident that he was unconvinced.

The following morning, at their regular 8:15 meeting to share job orders, Martin turned to Walter and said, "Walter has a JO he wants

[1]   The respondents in our mail survey reported that they had received an average (median) of sixty job orders during the first six months of 1995, of which they rated about half as "good" job orders (i.e., ones they had a reasonable probability of filling).

to let us know about." It was clear that the others knew what to expect because Martin's statement provoked an immediate response: "I bet it's Office Depot. Is it Office Depot?" Walter responded that Office Depot was looking for five loss-prevention managers, which provoked a flood of derisive comments: "You're joking," "Bullshit." Finally, Walter responded by saying, in a mock-aggrieved tone, "Oh, shut the fuck up." He continued, "Office Depot wants to do it right this time." Rhonda was in a bind, he argued, and was feeling the wrath of the operations VP. He relayed the contents of the conversation he had had with her, including his complaints about their hiring procedures and her acknowledgment that the round-robin approach would be scrapped. She had "guts," he said, for conceding that Office Depot's procedures were flawed, at which one of the headhunters interjected, "No, balls." Walter insisted, however, that Rhonda's admissions made the job orders worth pursuing.

Both then and afterward the other recruiters made it obvious that they had not been persuaded by Walter's arguments. Carl reminded Walter that he had sent the company fifteen LPM candidates and that not one had been hired. Later that day Carl explained that he would not send any LPM candidates to Office Depot because he was concerned about his reputation. When his candidates get rejected, they are as likely to blame him as the company, and the maintenance of a good reputation was of paramount importance for him: "I'm in this for the long haul." He had no confidence in the organization's procedures, despite what Rhonda was now saying: "It's like Charlie Brown and the football. Rhonda is Lucy."

This incident revealed how Walter's spin on the LPM job orders, because of his relationship with Office Depot, was completely different from that of the other headhunters in the firm. In effect, Walter was saying that he felt he could trust Office Depot to do the right thing, based on, first, the overall strength of his relationship with the company, which surely would eventually translate into success in filling LPM positions; second, his understanding of internal organizational relationships, that is, the pressure the VP was placing on Rhonda; and third, her apparent statement that the flaws in Office Depot's hiring process would be corrected. For the other headhunters, who did not have a close relationship with the company, these job orders were evaluated according to standard decision rules and were consequently viewed as unacceptable. As a footnote to this incident, it should be mentioned that when we checked a month later to see how Walter was progressing, none of his LPM candidates had received an offer.

Client Evaluation

Headhunters also apply a set of decision rules to evaluate the strength and quality of their relationships with their clients. Like assignment evaluations, these client assessments allow headhunters to figure out how likely it is they will make a placement. Headhunters use two criteria in particular to rate their client relationships: exclusivity and responsiveness. Exclusivity is a structural feature of the client-headhunter relationship whereas responsiveness is the headhunter's assessment of the behavior of the client during the search process.

Exclusivity refers to how many headhunters are seeking to fill the job order. Obviously, the fewer the number of competitors a headhunter has, the more likely she will make the placement, so headhunters prefer searches in which they have few if any rivals. Headhunters assume they will face stiff competition working on cold call–generated job orders whereas a client who calls them is unlikely to have offered the job order to numerous headhunters. (Although sometimes, headhunters report, employers go on "shopping" expeditions or use a "shotgun" approach and contact many headhunters about a search.)

When they receive a job order from a prospective client, therefore, one of the first questions headhunters ask is how many other headhunters have been given this assignment. The answer dictates the intensity with which they will conduct the search. Although all headhunters agree that the greater the number of competitors the less attractive the job order, there is no consensus on how many headhunters seeking to make the same placement push it beyond the limits of acceptability. For some headhunters, these bounds are very narrow. One said that if there were more than two headhunters plus himself working on a job order, he would not accept it. Some reach their limit at five or seven, and others do not object to competing with ten or twelve. Whatever the limit, when it is reached, the client effectively loses its client status with the headhunter, which means that the headhunter will downgrade the search from priority to perfunctory. Martin explained that if he felt there were too many headhunters competing for a job order, "you just kind of stick it [the job order] in the book and say, 'If you find anyone, guys, send it there, but we're not going to work real hard for that.' "

A headhunter reaches the pinnacle of exclusivity when she is the only one to be offered the job order. These searches are known as exclusives, and they may last from a few days to a few weeks, during which time, at least in theory, the client will not consider candidates from other headhunters who may have learned of the search and submitted candidate résumés. An exclusive or near-exclusive (i.e., one or two competitors only) makes an enormous difference in how headhunters conduct their business. Instead of just checking their data banks to see whether they have any qualified candidates on file and then submitting those résumés, they go all out to find the best candidates for the job.

There is considerable variation in the percentage of their business that headhunters report as consisting of exclusives. Barbara, who places people who work in physicians' offices, said she had never had an exclusive whereas Lisa said that about 60 percent of her business was made of up exclusives. Our rough estimate is that 10 to 20 percent of the job orders of the headhunters we interviewed were exclusives.

Headhunters who receive exclusive search assignments from clients herald the strength and importance of these relationships. Stan, an owner-manager of a nine-headhunter firm that places accountants and bookkeepers, declared, "On those assignments that we have where we are the only one they're working with and they need to fill it and they're giving us information, it's a beautiful relationship—it's just like the textbook would have." An exclusive allows the headhunter to devote himself or herself single-mindedly to the attempt to make the placement, knowing that a client who honors this arrangement will not entertain candidate résumés from other headhunters.

Responsiveness refers to how much information and feedback clients provide headhunters and to whether clients hire headhunters' candidates. Responsiveness is especially vital to headhunters when working with a new client because they are unlikely to be familiar with the client's organizational culture or the factors and procedures shaping its hiring decisions. A headhunter does not put as much effort or attention into a search for a client that fails to provide adequate feedback or hire the headhunter's candidates as he does for one that is perceived to be more forthcoming and cooperative.

Information means what clients tell candidates about the job order: an unresponsive client may offer little more than a job title and starting salary whereas a responsive client gives the headhunter some guidance for the search, such as the typical daily activities to be performed by the position's occupant, the performance expectations attached to the position, and if appropriate, an explanation why the position is open. Michelle emphasized that specific information was critical for undertaking the search: "If they [clients] can't be specific with their needs, there's red flags going up all over the place and I'll tell them, I'll say, 'Look, why don't I check back with you in a day or two and this will give you time to find out some of these really important bits of information that I need in order to be effective for you.'"

Feedback, as the term implies, means how clients respond once the search is under way, such as whether clients set up interviews with candidates who have been presented and how quickly and in how much detail they let headhunters know the results of interviews. A client who responds slowly or, worse still, makes no response when a headhunter presents a candidate is automatically demoted in the headhunter's eyes. George said, "If I do a lot of work and the guy [the client] doesn't call me back and kind of drags me and doesn't return any of my calls, the chances are I drop it right there."

In addition to noting how long it takes a client to return phone calls, headhunters have various tricks they can use, as Karen put it, to "test the opening and see if they [clients] are real serious about hiring someone rather than wasting my time." One stratagem is to present just one candidate to the client as a test case. If the client responds favorably albeit without hiring the candidate—if the client lets the headhunter know why the candidate was not interviewed or, if interviewed, was not hired—the search intensifies and other candidates are presented. If the client responds unfavorably—does not explain the interviewing or hiring decision—the search effort is scaled back if not abandoned altogether. Brian clearly expressed the test-case role of the single candidate:

> Let's say it's a new company that calls me and they say, "Hey, we need a production supervisor." Well, if it's a new company, I don't know them. . . . First, I search my database and if I have somebody there I'll call them and qualify the candidate. If not,

then I'll recruit. And then what I do is I like to try and give them a good candidate or two or three in front of them. And then I stop. I see how they respond. If they sort of dillydally or they say, "Well, we haven't had a chance to look at them yet" or "Oh, Joe's out of town and hasn't had a chance to look at it," then I'll begin to realize, hey, Brian, just hold on, you know. Feedback from my client is what gets me going more than anything else. Even if it's bad feedback, even if they tell me this candidate you sent us does not have just what we're looking for, that's okay. At least then I can tailor my search efforts to what they need. But if a client is just sort of wishy-washy and so forth, then I'll begin to sort of, I may recruit some, but maybe just in my spare time or you just sort of keep your eyes open or something like that.

Testing a client in this manner is similar to what occurs when a large company decides to try out a new supplier or service provider. To assess the provider's responsiveness and trustworthiness, the company places an initial order for a relatively small or unimportant item or service. If the test is passed, more crucial items or services may be ordered, gradually tightening the relationship between the two parties (Smitka 1991). In our case it is the service providers who are using this process of trial and error to gauge the interest and commitment of their more powerful clients.

The ultimate test of a client's responsiveness, as far as any headhunter is concerned, is hiring that headhunter's candidates. A client that does so can expect a wholehearted effort from the headhunter on subsequent searches. Conversely, if a headhunter is unsuccessful with her candidates, a subsequent assignment from that client may receive cursory or no attention.

A headhunter who receives exclusive assignments from responsive clients has achieved what Wayne Baker (1990) and others have referred to as a "relationship interface." Headhunters continually stress the value of these relationships, and yet they are a mixed blessing. An irony of headhunting is that the more successful headhunters are in creating strong relationships with clients, the more dependent the headhunters become on these clients. Dependence, in turn, is accompanied by vulnerability and insecurity.

The Problems of Dependence

Success for a headhunter means establishing strong client relationships. Nevertheless, these relationships create two problems for a headhunter. First, a headhunter who concentrates her efforts on recruiting for one or two good clients will be much more adversely affected by the loss of a client than would a headhunter who has weak ties with a wide range of clients. This problem has been characterized as the "paradox of embeddedness" (Uzzi 1997). Second, headhunters assume that the closer the relationship with a client, the greater the pressure they will be under to cut fees and the greater the temptation for the client to behave opportunistically.

The Paradox of Embeddedness

A nearly constant refrain among headhunters is that theirs is a "relationship-driven business." In their interviews with us and when we observed them at conferences and seminars they repeatedly emphasized the need to build and nurture their relationships with clients. Among the strategies we heard recommended were calling clients every sixty to ninety days, sending birthday cards to clients, and visiting clients' offices. The accounts headhunters relate of how they acquired particular clients usually feature the prominent role of networks of relationships: "I had developed a relationship with person A, and he/she suggested I call person B."

In our mail survey of Southern City headhunters we asked them how many "regular" clients they had. (Regular was defined as "clients for whom you have made multiple placements in the past and whom you expect to service in the future.") The median number of regular clients was fifteen. Within this group there is generally a smaller subset of clients that provide the bulk of a headhunter's job orders (and, therefore, fees). For example, Forrest said his firm did 95 percent of its business with its five largest clients. Dennis, a solo practitioner who specialized in the transportation industry, reported that in 1994 he had done business with seven different clients, two of which "represented the majority of the money that we made." It is quite common for recruiters to get 50 percent or more of their fees in any given year from a single client.

Job orders from regular clients are, therefore, critical to headhunters' economic fortunes. As Larry put it, "The cost of getting new business as opposed to repeat business is very high. Very high!" By relying heavily on one or two clients, however, a headhunter risks losing a substantial portion of his income if a client stops hiring or decides to use another headhunter. A company hiring freeze, for example, can be devastating for a headhunter who has become dependent on that client. Ben explained that he had been doing 75 percent of his business with Coca-Cola Foods until the company introduced a hiring freeze in 1994 that lasted thirteen months. He continued:

> The problem is that you become fat and happy dealing with two, three, four people, and should that business dry up, you're sitting there with your butt in your hand, per se. Meaning you have no business left. . . . So last year was kind of a good thing for me because it was a kind of kick in the butt, that you need to go out there and whether you have business or not, you need to go out there and keep pounding the phone until you make your phone calls.

Any headhunter with a large percentage of his business from one or two clients has a dilemma: not only is it far more pleasant to field phone calls from established clients than it is to make cold calls but the demands of doing a good job for one's established clients by conducting wide-ranging and thorough searches often allow little time for generating new business.

The danger of overreliance on one or two clients becomes just as apparent should a client switch headhunters. Although a switch may occur for many reasons, headhunters particularly fear the consequences of a personnel change at the client. Client-headhunter relationships are relationships between individuals rather than organizations. A headhunter's ties are usually to just a single individual within a single department of the client organization; should that person leave, there is no guarantee that her successor will continue to use the old headhunter. The loss of business because of the loss of the contact person was repeatedly cited by headhunters as a primary concern when they reviewed the relationships they had forged with clients. Larry succinctly summarized the individualistic component of client-headhunter relationships:

> Now you always have to get more companies because eventually that account will dry up. Because, what is an account? It's

not Pizza Hut. It's Bob Jones, the regional vice president. If Bob Jones leaves, the next guy comes in and says, "[Employment] agencies, I hate them!" Doesn't matter what you've done with that company before. If you can't convince them, "Hey, here's what it is," you'll lose that account.

The importance of individual attachments within headhunter-client relationships is consistent with provider-client ties in other settings, such as auditor-client relationships (Levinthal and Fichman 1988; Seabright, Levinthal, and Fichman 1992).

In short, building relationships with a few clients is the key to successful headhunting, but it also makes headhunters highly dependent on these clients. When headhunters establish these relationships, they mortgage their futures to the continuation of these ties. Success leads to dependence, and dependence in turn breeds vulnerability. Uzzi coined the term *paradox of embeddedness* to characterize what happens when a contractor in the apparel industry suffers the ending of a relationship with a client: "The embedded relationship that had originally benefitted the contractor may now put it at a higher risk of failure than if it had diversified its ties" (1997, 57). As we have shown, the paradox is equally apparent in headhunting.

Power and Mistrust

Social psychologists have long asserted the reciprocity of power and dependence: the dependence of one party provides the basis for the power of the other (e.g., Emerson 1962; Cook and Emerson 1984). The power of clients over headhunters is displayed in the pressure they exert to cut fees and in headhunters' fear of client disloyalty.

The fees headhunters charge clients vary somewhat, typically ranging from 20 to 35 percent of the new hire's first year's salary. But when they acquire regular clients, few headhunters are able to maintain their standard rates: they discover that their clients expect to receive a discount. Most headhunters accept this loss as an inevitable cost of client development. For example, Doug noted that his standard fee was 35 percent. He had recently, however, developed a strong relationship with a human resources manager at one of his clients and conducted a series of searches for the company for which he had agreed to accept a 25 percent fee.

One response to fee-cutting pressures is to request an exclusive. George indicated how he would negotiate with an employer who sought a fee discount, nicely illustrating the discount-exclusive quid pro quo: "You want a reduced rate—everybody wants a deal, right—so I'll say, okay, I'm going to do it for less, but I want an exclusive for a sixty-day period or whatever." Others accept low fees as the price for doing repeat business. For example, Gail said she was willing to accept a 15 percent fee "because I'm going to get repeat business during the course of the year. That's more important to me than having to keep that pipeline going with new business."

Not surprisingly, headhunters often resent fee-cutting clients, even when they get exclusives or repeat business, because lower fees represent both a loss of earnings and an undervaluation of headhunters' work. Ted, an engineering headhunter, even declared that he preferred to deal with new companies rather than established clients because when it came to the latter,

> the cozier you get with them, the more likelihood they're going to take advantage, in my opinion. If you make multiple placements with them, they'll want discounts. "Oh, Ted, you charged blah, blah for that placement, and I think this next time it should be 5 percent less, 10 percent less, blah, blah, blah." [All this was said in a whiny, high-pitched voice intended to mimic and mock the client.] But if it's a new company you're dealing with, you don't get that. . . . They have less respect for you in my opinion if you get too cozy and comfy.

Few headhunters that we spoke with took quite so bleak a view of their long-time clients, but it was evident to us from attending gatherings of headhunters and from reading trade publications such as the *Fordyce Letter* that complaints about fees figure prominently in headhunters' thinking. For example, at one conference we attended a roundtable session called "Fees: How to Negotiate, How to Structure." The nine headhunters at the table quickly launched into a lively discussion about acceptable and unacceptable fees. One headhunter, Cheryl, after listening to the discussion leader, Lisa, declare that her bottom line on fees was 20 percent, presented her problem to the group. She had a client that refused to pay more than a 15 percent fee on its job orders but was willing to make them exclusives. She wondered whether she should accept them, and she expressed ignorance of the "rules of thumb" for these cases, even though, as she noted, she had been doing recruiting for ten years. Only one person in the group, Dennis, had a straightforward answer for her: in his view it was bad practice to concede to lower fees. Others were far more equivocal. Lisa's response was that if the headhunter gave value to a client, the client would pay a reasonable fee, without indicating whether 15 percent was reasonable or not. She also acknowledged, somewhat contradictorily, that in Cheryl's specialty, office-staff recruiting, "everyone negotiates." Another headhunter, Justin, suggested that she use her candidates as a bargaining chip—let the client know she had good candidates but make it clear that the client would have to pay full fee to see them. Cheryl did not respond to this advice directly but instead told an unrelated story of a dispute she was having with Turner Broadcasting over the payment of a fee.

The problem that Cheryl and other headhunters in her position face is that they are to a certain degree victims of their own success. When they establish close ties with a small number of clients, they stake their futures on the continuation of these relationships. No headhunter wants to lose a client that provides a significant portion of her revenue, so they are placed on a defensive, concession-granting footing. The fact that it is far more consequential for a headhunter to lose a client than it is for a client to lose its headhunter gives clients the upper hand in negotiations between the parties.

The contest between headhunters and their clients over fees underscores for many headhunters the adversarial dimension of their relationship. It fuels a sense of inequity and betrayal, which often emerges in conversations about clients. Significantly, it is when the headhunter-client relationship is at its strongest—when headhunters are given exclusive search assignments—that they express their gravest doubts about their clients' integrity. Headhunters believe clients have the incentive and the opportunity to behave opportunistically toward them.

Headhunters recognize and fear that clients have powerful motives to get headhunters to commit to intensive search efforts, promising them exclusive or near-exclusive assignments but at the same time considering candidates submitted by other headhunters. Stan remarked: "They [clients] can tell you all you want about how much they love you and how they hate a different recruiter. . . . If a résumé comes across their desk from their most hated person, they'll look at it." A client who is willing to consider résumés from headhunters who have not been offered the assignment gets the best of both worlds: the uninhibited efforts of a headhunter who believes himself to be engaged in an exclusive search and the possibly better candidates produced by rival headhunters eager to break up the exclusive relationship. Headhunters simply do not believe clients who claim they do not look at unsolicited résumés.

In making this argument we wish to emphasize two points. First, not every headhunter we interviewed questioned his or her client's fidelity. Nevertheless, this concern arose with sufficient regularity in our interviews and at our fieldwork sites to lead us to conclude that it was widespread. More important, the remarks were unsolicited and were made, in most instances, by some of the most experienced headhunters we interviewed; client disloyalty had not been one of our initial interview topics. Second, we do not suggest that all clients are as unfaithful as these comments may indicate. Our claim is that headhunters make the assumption of client infidelity—based, quite possibly, on a few incidents—which then shapes how they think and act about clients. A statement by Ted exemplifies headhunters' concerns about opportunistic behavior by clients:

> I do know you can't trust them. Absolute statement—there's no loyalty, and I just assume there's no loyalty and no trust. If there is, I lucked out; it's a bonus. But they're going to be saying, they're going to give the impression that they're working only with me, when they're really working with several simultaneously. They want to get the job filled as soon as possible; they'll do whatever is necessary to do it, even if it means lying, like, for example, a company tells me I'm working an assignment on an exclusive basis.

Headhunters fear that regardless of how good their relationship is with a client, and even if they are engaged in an exclusive search, the client could hire a candidate provided by another headhunter. It is through painful experience—the "ninth-inning placement from some other source," as Frank put it—that headhunters "learn the hard way" that they need to be aware of the possibility of client opportunism.

The issues we have identified here—headhunter vulnerability and their mistrust of clients—are not found in all client-provider relationships. For instance, Robert Faulkner's (1983) study of Hollywood composers found that filmmakers' power, based on their control over the allocation of work to composers, was counterpoised by their need to hire the top composers to lessen the risks associated with movie production. To take another example, Andrea Larson's analysis of the dyadic relationships between high-growth entrepreneurial firms and their partners (suppliers, distributors, or customers) revealed an absence of opportunism and the predominance of "norms of fairness, honesty, and reciprocity" (1992, 96).

Part of the explanation for the differences between these relationships and the one between headhunters and their clients can be found in Burt's (1992) structural-hole theory. Headhunters are an example of players in a relationship who have low "structural autonomy" because they are easily replaced by other, more-or-less identical players who surround them. A client who considers résumés submitted by headhunters with whom it does not have a relationship confirms the replaceability of all contingency headhunters. In Burt's terminology, headhunters are redundant players because they are so easily substitutable (1992, 40–42). Composers, in contrast, are not so easily substituted for one another. Unlike the situation in headhunting, there is no contingency arrangement that allows a client to share an assignment with more than one provider at no cost. Further, as we have already noted, filmmakers have strong incentives to have their films scored by only the best-known composers. Similarly, the partnerships Larson observed are by definition relationships in which both parties are nonredundant.

Even nonredundant players, however, may be tempted to behave opportunistically if they believe it will confer an advantage. Larson's study explains why this may or may not happen. The network dyads were founded on the basis of "prior personal relationships": the partnerships were formed because the leaders of the two companies involved knew each other well, and the experience of working together consolidated and strengthened their preexisting ties. The relationships, therefore, were socially embedded at the outset and became increasingly embedded over time, providing the preconditions under which honesty and loyalty were likely to flourish. Such preconditions are largely absent from client-headhunter relationships. Most notably, embeddedness, which provides the basis for shared norms and enforceable trust, is weak.

Reciprocal Opportunism

Burt has argued that players may be able to blunt the impact of low structural autonomy by reaching agreement with their competitors not to allow themselves to be played against one another (1992, 72). This "oligopoly strategy" is not feasible, however, in the atomized world of headhunting, where not only are barriers to entry minimal but rival headhunters may not even be aware of one another's existence. Instead, headhunters have developed a strategy of reciprocal opportunism: they have decided that it is acceptable under certain circumstances to be disloyal and even dishonest in their dealings with clients. This strategy is most visible when headhunters recruit candidates from firms that are their clients, a clear violation of one of the cardinal principles of headhunting. Reciprocal opportunism delimits the loyalty of headhunters to clients by establishing the conditions under which it is permissible to recruit from clients.

Firms from which headhunters may not recruit candidates are said to be "off limits." The most common reason a firm is off limits is that the headhunter placed a candidate there—it is a client. Without exception, all the headhunters to whom we spoke said they had off-limits policies, and they firmly condemned "front door/back door recruiting," or placing one candidate with a client while recruiting someone else out of the same firm for another client. Clients, as might be expected, were even more adamant. As one said, "You know the old adage: you're not a source and a client. I take that very seriously."

Off-limits policies would seem to require headhunters to evince a high degree of loyalty and constraint, but in practice they circumvent these policies—and their commitment to clients—in three ways. First, headhunters argue that the client is really a subunit or person within the organization in which they have made placements rather than the organization as a whole. Second, they maintain that a client is someone for whom they have made a placement relatively recently—within the previous year, for example. Both rationalizations seek to narrow the definition of a client, that is, to show that an organization that may appear to be a client is not really one. Third, headhunters argue that if an employee from a client approaches them, they are then free to place that employee with another firm. Taking a self-initiated candidate out of a client, they reason, does not violate the off-limits policy because the candidate has implicitly taken responsibility for his or her job change.

The client-is-a-person argument is a reflection of the fact, as we noted earlier, that a headhunter's relationship with a client is often just a relationship with a contact person—the hiring manager—at the client's firm. This has two implications. First, other hiring managers within the firm likely have relationships with other headhunters. Second, if the contact leaves, the headhunter is in danger of losing his or her client. The headhunter-client relation is thus both individualized and fragmented. Headhunters, in response, restrict their loyalty to the positions for which the contact is responsible. Doug forcefully articulated this circumscribed definition of a client:

> A client is somebody like my relationship with Jane Brown at Meade. Somebody that we've developed a relationship with and I am her primary recruiter, if not her exclusive recruiter. It's not going to behoove me to go in and take somebody out of Jane's organization as far as Meade Coated Board. Now, there are even within Meade Coated Board, there are areas. She handles just the marketing and sales arena. So she is my client for that arena. Now, the paper mill itself and other divisions of Meade are fair game. And they use other recruiters. And they don't use me. So to me, Meade as a corporation is not the client. Jane Brown and Meade Coated Board, or really sales and marketing, is my client. So that's how I define it.

The argument that a client is someone with whom a headhunter has made a recent placement reflects the fact that even under the best of circumstances a headhunter's prospects of continuing to make placements with a particular client are uncertain. A firm that has been a very good client may impose a hiring freeze, for example. Another client may decide to bypass its established relationship with a headhunter and give or at least share its business with other headhunters. Headhunters operationalize recency in two ways. First, they set a time limit—the most typical is twelve months—within which, if they have not made a placement at a particular firm, it is no longer considered a client. Second, they insist that a client must be a company with which they have actually made a placement rather than one that has provided them just the opportunity of making a placement. For a firm merely to give a headhunter a search assignment does not make it a client because headhunters claim that companies sometimes hand out "phantom" assignments to protect themselves from being "raided." Henry declared: "A client is a person whose check lands here, and it better be a check every couple of years at least or they're not a client any longer." In other words, a client that does not maintain its relationship is liable to be raided for candidates.

Off-limits policies are skirted and loyalty compromised most commonly when a candidate who works for a client, or who may even have been placed with the client by the headhunter, approaches the headhunter about changing employers. These cases represent the most severe test of a headhunter's loyalty because the headhunter cannot claim that the client is not really a client. Loyalty would require the headhunter to refuse to accept all candidates from client firms, including those who have approached the headhunter at their own volition. We found only one headhunter who had adopted such an unequivocal position, largely on practical grounds. Scott reasoned that if he declined to place a client-based candidate, once this person had left the organization (through some other means) he would get the assignment of finding a replacement and his loyalty would be rewarded with still more business from the client.

The other headhunters felt they were entitled to take a candidate out a client firm, provided the candidate approached them first. The most difficult of these cases are candidates who were placed by headhunters and later approach the same headhunters about getting out. Headhunters justify their "re-recruitment" of these candidates—a practice also known as "burning and churning"—by specifying criteria additional to the main one of the candidate's making the initial contact. For example, a headhunter may insist that the candidate remain in the job for at least twelve months before the headhunter will find her another job. A headhunter may require the candidate to make some effort to resolve his difficulties with his supervisor. In the final analysis, however, headhunters view the employment relationship as a contract in which each side has rights and obligations. If an employer does not meet an employee's expectations concerning salary increases or career advancement, many headhunters feel they should help that employee change jobs. Dale explained:

Now, my own personal opinion is that if a candidate approaches us . . . and [has] heard that we have an opening that they want to pursue, for whatever reason—better career, closer to home, more money, bigger challenge, who knows—and I have done everything that I possibly could to salvage that relationship with the client, then I feel like I've got an obligation not only to my client to help them find people, but also to the candidates in the industry to help them pursue their career goals. I mean, it's a two-way street, you know.

Ray offered a specific example of a case in which he felt justified in finding a new position for a candidate he had already placed once because it was what the candidate wanted:

> I had a woman I recruited from Sovereign Bank in Virginia. This was a search assignment I got with Trust Company Bank right when I first moved down here. Placed her in a Trust tax manager's role. Pretty significant size position, and nine months into it she called me up and said: "You put me in here. You get me out." I mean, she hated it. And I got on the phone and made phone calls all over the place. I determined at that point, based on what she told me, we sat down and talked, that Trust Company wasn't the type of, or this particular department at Trust Company wasn't a department that I was going to be looking to get more business out of. And I felt like I owed her. She was miserable. And I placed her down with First Union in Florida. So some people can look at me and say, well, I made two fees off the same woman within a year with two different companies and it's burning and churning. But I didn't go back to her and say, "I've got this great opportunity."

Dale's comment about helping candidates achieve their career goals and Ray's observation that he did not expect the Trust Company to be a long-term client illustrate the pragmatic flexibility that headhunters see as necessary for their survival in their competitive environment. Headhunters, as we have noted, are agents of clients and are paid by them. In matching client and candidate, the headhunter normally represents the client. But there are occasions when headhunters feel justified in switching sides, in effect becoming the candidate's agent and thereby violating the off-limits rule. The immediate rationalization for this change of loyalties may be the fact that the candidate initiated the contact; the underlying rationalization, however, is the headhunter's suspicion of his clients' motives and behavior and his consequent feeling that the occasional disloyal and opportunistic action he commits simply helps even the score.

Reciprocal opportunism demonstrates that headhunters, who operate in a highly competitive market without the advantages of client dependence or enforceable trust, are not powerless. Notwithstanding their weak structural position and lack of embedded ties, they assert some amount of control over their environment through their management of clients. By establishing exclusive ties with clients or behaving opportunistically toward them, headhunters act to reduce their dependence, or in the language of the structural-holes argument, to increase their structural autonomy.

5

Ruses, Pitches, and Wounds

The Construction of Job Candidates

> A lot of people, a lot of people are content but not necessarily
> happy where they are.
>
> —Martin, A Southern City headhunter

In his afterword to *Getting a Job* Granovetter observes that the most common way of finding a job is through not searching for that or any other job. He adds that little is known about nonsearch job acquisition, however, since most models of this behavior assume an active searcher. He then suggests that "finding a job without a search may be close to a proxy for finding a job through personal contacts" (1995, 145). Another possibility is that nonsearchers are recruited by headhunters. Candidate recruitment is central to the three issues with which this book is concerned: the value of headhunters as third-party brokers linking employers and candidates, the process by which headhunters convert nonsearchers into job candidates, and the criteria headhunters use in selecting and screening candidates. In this chapter we focus on the first two issues, leaving the third for the next chapter.

A critical difference between personal contacts and headhunters lies in their relationship to job candidates. Contacts want to help particular candidates find jobs with little or no thought of the benefits to themselves. Headhunters have little or no commitment to any single candidate since their overriding concern is to find candidates—any candidates—to fill positions so they can earn commissions from their clients. Headhunters are salespeople, and like other salespeople, they aim to discover prospects and convert them into customers. As various studies of salesworkers have observed, the process of selling involves learning how to manipulate the emotions of others, exploit social relationships for financial gain, and assert control over conversations and other interactions with prospects (Dorsey 1994;

Hochschild 1983; Leidner 1993; Oakes 1990; Prus 1989a). All these aspects are found in headhunting, but the headhunter-candidate relationship is different from other provider-customer relationships in one critical respect: headhunters have two sets of customers, employers *and* candidates, and their relationships with each are radically dissimilar.

In their relationships with employers, as seen in the previous chapter, headhunters pursue the conventional sales strategy of attempting to turn prospects into customers and then into clients. Their goal is to develop long-term associations that will generate repeat business, at the same time minimizing the risks of becoming too dependent on any one client. With candidates, however, headhunters must forge a series of one-time connections since it is not customary for a candidate to be placed more than once by the same headhunter. Further, in contrast to customers in other settings, candidates do not pay for the service they are provided, which means they lack the economic ties to headhunters that customers and their service providers normally have. Headhunters, it is worth reiterating, work for employers not candidates, and they represent the interests of the former not the latter. Finally, headhunters must not only persuade candidate prospects to become customers, or buyers (i.e., job candidates); they must also persuade these the same prospects to sell themselves when they go on job interviews—this is the double sale that is the defining feature of headhunting. The result is that headhunters have an even weaker hand when prospecting for candidates than they do when dealing with employers.

For many headhunters, finding job candidates is more difficult than finding clients because employers, under most circumstances, have some interest in finding new employees (although they may not be willing to entrust the task of finding these employees to the headhunter who has contacted them); prospective job candidates, in contrast, may have little or no interest in making a job change. A reality of headhunting is that the people who make the best candidates are not generally active job seekers. Headhunters find these people and turn them into candidates through a combination of persistence, persuasion, manipulation, and deception that draws on all their conversational quick-wittedness. They have to talk and trick their way into learning the names of prospects, and they have to coax and maneuver these prospects into becoming candidates. Getting job candidates is a four-stage process. First, headhunters must identify people who are likely to qualify as candidates. Second, they must contact these prospects and "pitch" the opportunity to them. Third, headhunters must decide, once they have candidates interested in the position, whether they are in fact qualified and, if so, whether they should be "presented" to an employer. Fourth, headhunters must locate the "wounds" candidates have that will lead them to welcome a job change.

Naming Names: The Process of Candidate Identification

Headhunters find candidates in various ways and in various places. Some are found in the candidate databases that every headhunter maintains. Others are found through networking: someone in the headhunter's circle of acquaintances tells her that this person in that company might be a strong candidate for the position for which she is recruiting. Still others are found through cold calls: the headhunter calls blindly into a particular company hoping to find someone who would be qualified for and interested in the position.

Database Searches
  In the easiest (and cheapest) form of candidate search a headhunter simply looks through her database for someone who qualifies for the position in question. The people whose names appear in these databases fall into two broad categories. Some are people with whom the headhunter has spoken in the past, when engaged in other searches or when seeking job orders. Headhunters spend an enormous amount of time on the telephone in pursuit of clients and candidates. Their efforts are mostly unsuccessful, in the sense that the probability that any one call will lead to an immediate job order or a qualified candidate is low. The people contacted, however, enter headhunters' databases as potential clients or potential candidates or both. A determined headhunter thus will not be discouraged if she calls someone who immediately says he is not interested in the position for which she is recruiting; instead, she will inquire about his education, job title and responsibilities, salary (usually asked in the form of a range), work history, willingness to relocate, what he would consider an ideal opportunity, career aspirations, his marital status, and, if he's married, what his wife does. As Rich explained, "When you make a call, you're investing your quarter, so get something for your quarter. Every time you make a call, get something." Eric said:

I look at every conversation as a potentially good conversation and try to get something out of it. I mean, if the guy's not right for this job, then hey, maybe he's right for something I'm going to get next week. And I want to understand him a little better, and I want to leave him with a feeling that I was good to him, that he had a positive experience, and that he will be willing to come back, and that if I ring the phone again, he will come back, willingly.

The second category of people in the databases are those who have contacted the headhunter themselves. They may have submitted their résumés in response to a newspaper or online ad the headhunter ran (some headhunters maintain Web sites where they list positions for which they are seeking candidates), or perhaps they were referred to the headhunter by a friend or acquaintance. Not all headhunters are eager to enlarge their databases through candidate-initiated or unsolicited contact; the headhunters who rely on this form of recruitment tend to be those who fill lower-level positions in the local Southern City labor market. For example, Stan, who has an eight-headhunter firm that places accountants and bookkeepers, puts an ad in the major city newspaper each Sunday. On a recent Sunday (April 2, 2000) his firm advertised eleven positions, including a staff accountant ($35,000), a senior tax analyst ($46,000 and bonus), and a plant controller ($65,000). Other headhunters who use ads and/or referrals are those who place nurses and medical office staff, secretaries and office-support personnel, paralegals and other legal staff, and dental hygienists.

As a general rule, headhunters who rely on ads or referrals to expand their candidate databases are engaged in low-level and/or routine searches in which the qualifications for the position are relatively straightforward. These headhunters use their large, comprehensive, and up-to-date databases to screen and identify candidates almost instantaneously. George explained that his database of 15,000 to 16,000 candidates enabled his firm to conduct extraordinarily rapid and thorough searches. He said that if he was contacted by a client in the morning, "I can have you people this afternoon; process will be rolling tomorrow." He continued:

We're in the business to track people that are perfect. To get you whatever you want: you want an MBA, you want a CPA, you want a person out of a certain school, certain GPA, we can run people by GPA, certain computer skills, certain acquisition skills, certain treasury skills, cash skills—I mean, you name it. Whatever skill on your résumé, risk management, you name it. I mean, I can find anybody I want.

The database approach to finding candidates assumes that candidates are relatively easily obtainable—they just need to be identified. It also assumes that the client has provided clearly specified and unambiguous search parameters. In many searches, however, neither of these assumptions holds. One problem is that qualified candidates may be hard to find. Ray pointed out that it was not a problem to locate an accountant who was a CPA and had three to five years of experience; finding an accountant with international financial experience was considerably more difficult: "These type of people are not necessarily sitting in everybody's drawer, and it's going to take some real detective work to go out and find that person."

The people in the databases, particularly those who respond to the ads, are often unqualified for the hard-to-fill positions—the same problem that employers face when they place ads. Further, even if qualified, a candidate may still fall well short of an employer's hiring criteria. Such mismatches occur because ads list a position's specs alone whereas employers actually hire those candidates with whom they have the best chemistry. Take, for example, an ad for a financial analyst found on the RSC Web site:

> Individual will provide financial analyses and support in finance and accounting areas. Responsibilities include forecasting, cost analysis, budgeting, control evaluation, and various accounting and finance duties. Analysis duties involve tracking, reporting, and evaluating field and home office financial data. Directly assists VP of Finance by reporting trends, assisting in financial decisions, and performing a variety of different projects and projections. Ideal candidate will have strong administrative, organization, and communication skills, a degree in Accounting, and 3+ years of related experience. CPA and/or CFA preferred.

This ad is simply an itemization of the position's specifications, albeit a fairly detailed one, and it offers prospective applicants little guidance about the factors that will tilt the hiring decision in favor of one candidate rather than another. In the following chapter we explore at length what these factors are and how headhunters find out about them. The point we wish to emphasize here is that satisfying a position's specs provides no assurance that a candidate will meet an employer's desires.

Another problem is that many employees are reluctant to respond to ads, and therefore are less likely to appear in databases, for fear that word will get back to the boss that they are on the job market. No employee wants to be perceived as disloyal—at least not until he or she has decided to quit. Ads typically do not indicate what company the position is with, so it takes an unusually brave or disgruntled employee to submit a résumé to an unfamiliar headhunter for a job with an unspecified organization. Employees who are concerned about confidentiality are similarly reluctant to list their résumés with online job-matching and job-finding services such as headhunter.net and monster.com (although headhunters still find these sites worth checking).

Consequently, most headhunters do not expect to find their best candidates through ads, in their databases, or on online job boards. Any or all of these may be used in the beginning stages of a search, but if, as expected, they do not produce the right candidates, the headhunter must turn to other means of finding them: drawing on his networks and cold-calling.

Network Searches

When headhunters begin to hunt down candidates who are not in their databases, they normally start by calling people they know who they think may be able to suggest a name or two. Typically, these contacts are former candidates whom the headhunter has placed and who perform the same or similar job to that for which the headhunter is now recruiting. A headhunter who is searching for, say, a chief financial officer for a retail firm, therefore, calls other CFOs in the retail sector. Particularly valuable are contacts who are a level above the position being recruited for because they are likely to know who the rising stars in the industry are. For example, Rich calls *chief* estimators when he is looking for estimator candidates. Using networks to find candidates has two main benefits. First, former placements are likely to be well disposed toward the headhunter who placed them and thus willing to offer some referrals. Second, headhunters

believe successful people—their contacts—tend to recognize and as-
sociate with other successful people in their field. "Birds of a feather
flock together, okay," was how Gail put it.

If asking a contact to refer someone just like herself fails to produce anyone who is willing to become a candidate, headhunters can
expand their network searches in a couple of ways. One is by trolling
their networks for contacts who work with the people who occupy
the positions for which they are recruiting. These contacts can be
asked to recommend someone they deal with regularly and find to be
highly competent. Scott explained this process, known as "backward
sourcing": "If I'm recruiting an insurance underwriter, who are the
people that day to day deal with that underwriter? It's the insurance
salesmen. So I'll call my salesmen and say, 'Who's your best underwriter and why is that person good?'"

The other option for a headhunter is to use her network of fellow
recruiters. Many recruiters belong to formal networks that have
arrangements for sharing job orders and candidates. A headhunter
who is unable to find a suitable candidate for a position may request
assistance from other members of her network; if one of them produces the candidate who is hired, the two headhunters split the
placement fee.

Cold-Calling

For most headhunters, however, referrals from their networks simply do not generate sufficient candidates for all their searches. Consequently, they have to cold-call prospective candidates. A good part of
the art of headhunting lies in knowing whom to call, how to get
through on the telephone, and what to say during this conversation;
headhunters must do all these things effectively if an employed
stranger is to be converted into an eager and viable job candidate.

How do headhunters know whom to call? Occasionally, they come
across the name of a possible candidate in a trade publication or a
news release (here the Internet is particularly useful). Headhunters
often join the associations of the industry in which they recruit, allowing them to attend national conventions and receive industry
magazines and newsletters. Far better than these publications, although much more difficult to obtain, are company directories,
which list employees by name and job title. We observed a number of
headhunters using directories. For example, we listened to Diane, a
Brown Recruiting headhunter who specializes in the beauty products

area, work her way down the brand managers in a Chesebrough-Pond's directory trying to find a candidate for Almay (although she didn't attract much interest in the job during the period we observed her). She had obtained the directory from a friend at Chesebrough-Pond's. Another BR headhunter, who recruits brand managers for consumer-package companies, proudly showed off Kraft and Nestlé directories he had acquired. The Kraft directory included home telephone numbers and addresses; the Nestlé directory was even more valuable because it showed job titles as well as the specific products for which the managers were responsible.

Most of the time, however, headhunters do not have directories of candidates. Instead, they have to rely on their wits and glibness of tongue to extract these names from organizational gatekeepers. The most straightforward way of doing this is for the headhunter to call the organization and ask for the occupant of the position in which he is interested. For example, a headhunter looking for a director of sales and marketing for a food-products company will call other food-products companies and ask to be put through to their directors of sales and marketing. A headhunter looking for a store manager for, say, a Regis store in Milwaukee will call other store managers at similar stores in the Milwaukee area. These calls have two purposes: to find out whether the recipient is interested in the position and, if not, to generate names of other prospective candidates. Headhunters are trying, in effect, to develop new contacts and break into their networks.

Although these calls sound simple, various complications often arise. One is that positions across organizations are not always equivalent. A search that was proving to be particularly difficult for RSC for exactly this reason was for a director of loss prevention and audit at L. Luria & Sons. Most companies like Luria separate the loss-prevention and auditing functions, so finding a candidate who had both in his or her background was proving to be frustrating. Jenny, the researcher[1] who was making the candidate calls, had taken to calling it "the auditor from hell" search. After making about twenty-five calls, she had found what she thought was the perfect candidate at Pep Boys (one of the few companies that combines LP and auditing), and

---

[1] A researcher searches for candidates, as any headhunter would do, but does not work with clients or arrange interviews between candidates and clients; once the candidates have been identified, the researcher turns their names over to a headhunter.

he seemed attracted by the offer because it would provide both a promotion and a salary increase; he said he needed to talk to his wife about the position, however, and now was not returning any of Jenny's calls. She had concluded that he was not interested, and she was back to cold-calling.

An even bigger problem, exactly the opposite of the one just described, occurs when any one organization has a surfeit of potential candidates. Most of the mid-level positions for which headhunters recruit—brand managers, loss-prevention managers, estimators, sales representatives, production supervisors, process engineers, project managers, underwriters, and the like—have multiple occupants. This situation creates considerable awkwardness for headhunters. It is one thing to call up a firm and ask for *the* director of sales and marketing or *the* regional loss-prevention manager and quite another to ask for *any* engineer or *any* sales representative. Organizational gatekeepers, such as receptionists and secretaries, are wary of headhunters at the best of times, and a vague request to be put through to the unspecified members of a particular department is sure to arouse their suspicions.

If a headhunter is lucky, his ignorance may go undetected. Rich pointed to a pile of résumés lying on his desk and explained his good fortune in getting them. As we have noted, he normally asks to speak to the chief estimator. In this case the chief estimator was not in, and in the subsequent conversation with a secretary he got a slew of other names. He recreated both sides of the conversation for us, beginning with the secretary's naming of the chief estimator:

> "Joe White is chief estimator."
> "May I speak with him?"
> "He's not in."
> "Who works with Joe?"
> "Sam Smith."
> "Okay, is he in?"
> "No, Sam's out also."
> "That's too bad." Small chitchat. "I'm having a hard time today, aren't I? Who else works with him? Why don't you just give me the list of them because I'll be calling back and we won't have to go through this name thing again. Who are the estimators in that department?" Sometimes the secretaries, if I

catch one who's new or not thinking, she'll give me a whole
list, and at my leisure I'll go back and I'll call each one.

Headhunters cannot count on strokes of luck, however. Instead, the
trick they must pull off, if they are to get through to prospects, is to
convince the gatekeepers that they are not headhunters and that they
actually know the person they wish to contact. Headhunters call this
"rusing." Denying that one is a headhunter is the most common
ruse. Among the identities headhunters assume are that of a student
writing a term paper, a writer for an industry newsletter, a secretary,
someone conducting a survey, a customer, and an insurance agent.

An example of the "conducting-a-survey" ruse are the calls that
Dawn, a researcher at BR, made when searching for process engineers
with refractination experience. All she had was the name of a company that was likely to have them. She began by calling the corporate
office of the target company, asking for the number of the polyethylene plant; when questioned as to her purpose, she replied: "I need to
send some information to the process engineers." She identified herself as "Karen" from "Quantum," a ruse that worked: she was given
the names and numbers of the technical supervisor (Jeff) and his secretary (Sandy) at the polyethylene plant. She then called Sandy, making sure to address her by name: "Hi, is this Sandy? Are you Jeff's secretary? What's your zip code? I'm from Quantum. I've sent stuff to
Jeff before, and I need to send him some more. I also need to send it to
some of the process engineers." Again, the ruse worked, and Sandy
provided names of engineers as well as a connection to another secretary, Pat. Dawn called Pat next: "Hi, Pat. I need to send stuff to the
area engineers over there who deal with the refractination process."
She got the names of two more process engineers in the polyethylene
plant from Pat. After she hung up, she explained that this call was a
good illustration of how she worked. At an earlier stage in her career
she might have not have been as persistent in trying to identify candidates with exactly the right qualifications, but she had learned it
was pointless to generate the names of people who weren't qualified.
By persevering, she had identified two engineers who met the specs.
Dawn also pointed out that these calls showed the value of talking
with secretaries: if you knew their names, they would assume it was
okay to talk with you, and they were an invaluable source of information about names, job titles, and lines of authority. Observing and

listening to Dawn, we were struck by how readily her ruse was acccpted: nobody asked her who "Quantum" was or what kind of survey or "stuff" she wanted to send to the engineers.

Marsha provided the following example of the "customer" ruse:

> I needed a purchaser for a manufacturing distributing company
> last month, and I needed these people from Rockwell. . . . Well,
> I needed to recruit these people today, and I told Robert [the in
> dustrial salesperson recruiter in her office] about the situation.
> That was at eleven o'clock in the morning. At one o'clock he
> came in my office and gave me the list. They faxed it over.
> That's how good he is.
>   Q: What was his trick?
>   He acted as if he were a company, and something had just
> fallen apart there, and he could not wait for them to send it,
> and he needed to talk—he did not know who to talk to, but if
> he had a list, he would know who to ask, because they needed
> the parts immediately before everything disintegrated.

A helpful receptionist had faxed him the list of names and job titles.
Headhunters may also be able to get names through voice mail. Although voice mail can be very frustrating for a headhunter trying to
get job orders, it can help one in search of candidates. Brian explained:

> One of the most wonderful things, tools for a recruiter . . . is
> some of these voice mail things, you know. I'll give you a per
> fect example—it's Frito-Lay. If you call into a Frito-Lay plant,
> they'll say, "For maintenance, press this button. For produc
> tion, press this button." Okay, let's say I want production. I
> press this button for production. Okay, "For Suzie Smith, press
> this. For Bob Jones, press this." Well, it just gives you a whole
> list of names of production supervisors. It's just a wonderful re
> cruiting tool. So that's easy, a piece of cake.

An alternative to asking for names is for the headhunter to pretend
to know the employee he is trying to contact. A headhunter will tell
the gatekeeper he is trying to reach an employee he met at a conference or restaurant but is unable to remember his name: "I was talking with a guy at Bennigan's at lunch a few days ago about software
issues. I really liked the guy, and I said that I'd give him a call later in

the week to talk more about computers. I've lost his name and number—he wrote them on a napkin—but I remembered that he worked for you folks." Of course, there was no meeting and there is no such employee. The headhunter will then offer a generic description of the mythical employee—five ten, brown hair and eyes, glasses, medium build—hoping the receptionist will say, "Oh, that sounds like so-and-so." The key to the forgotten-name ruse, as Gene, the owner-manager of Technology Services Associates, explained, is not to bite on the first name that is offered. Have the receptionist offer two or three names before accepting one. This tactic achieves two purposes. First, it adds credibility to the call because the caller is intentionally prolonging the conversation whereas a phony would presumably want to make it as short as possible. Second, it provides two additional names. The probability that any of the three employees will be right for the job for which the headhunter is recruiting is remote; their value is that they are the headhunter's port of entry to the organization. Karen said: "You go in there and call them, and they say, 'No, no, that doesn't fit me, but have you talked to so-and-so?' And you network like crazy; that one name leads to another."

The forgotten-name ruse may be employed in conjunction with the false-identity ruse. Brian talked about how he sometimes combined them when recruiting production supervisors:

> To me one of the hardest positions to recruit for, and one of the most common job orders I have, is for a production supervisor. Because you have this production plant, the facility, and the production supervisors are out in the plant. They may not have an office where they're sitting at the desk with a phone. And you have to be innovative, I mean, where you have to walk a fine line. I'll just give you an example of how I might do one. Let's say I'm looking for a production supervisor. Well, I'll call the company that I'm recruiting from, and I'll just simply say, "Production," okay. Sometimes you may get switched back to Production. Sometimes you may not. They may say, "Well, who do you want to talk to? We've got several production supervisors." That's where you have to try and be innovative. And I usually may say something like, "Well, you know, I was talking to one of the supervisors there earlier this morning, I can't remember his name. If you can just transfer me back to the Production area, I'm sure somebody back there will be able to pick

up." Well, sometimes you get right through. Well, they may
say, "Well, then, you know we have twenty-five supervisors
right there. I can't help you." Well, then you have to sort of,
"Okay, well, I'm with Aetna Insurance, and he was talking to
me about insurance. I do know he worked in the cookie area."

"Okay, well, let me transfer." Eventually you may get back
there.

Once a headhunter has a name, she can call the prospect. If, as
often happens, the employee is unavailable, she will have to decide
whether to leave a message or try again. In leaving a message, she is
likely to continue to conceal her identity and the purpose of her call.
For example, when Dawn was looking for process engineers, she
ended up in someone's voice mail, where she left the following message: "This is Dawn Jennings. My number is 1–800-###-####. I'm
calling about—" and then she hung up. She explained that she did it
to make the recipient curious—he would assume she must have been
cut off accidentally in the middle of the message and would be more
likely to return the call. Moreover, a 1–800 number wouldn't cost the
caller anything. She also said that when the 1–800 number rang in the
office, whoever answered it would not say, "Brown Recruiting," as
was done with the regular number, and the caller, therefore, would
not know he had just returned a call to a recruiter. Headhunters use
slightly different tactics if they are leaving a message with a person.
Karen said she would not identify herself as a recruiter if she were
leaving a message; she would just say she had met the person at a
conference and wanted to talk to him about a 401(k) issue. On other
occasions a headhunter may claim to be a friend of the employee he
is trying to contact, assuming that no receptionist or secretary will
question the friendship's authenticity. These ruses are not entirely
self-serving. Headhunters are aware that for any employee to be contacted by a headhunter is a mixed blessing: an employee's gratifica-
tion at being headhunted will be tempered by the realization that his
loyalty may be questioned should his contact with the headhunter
become known to his superiors.

Pitching the Job

A headhunter calls a prospect for three reasons. First, he wants to determine whether she is interested in the job and, if so, whether she

would make a viable candidate. Second, if, as is probable, she is not interested in the job, he wants her to supply the names of other prospects. Third, he wants to get more information about the prospect herself so he can add her to his database for subsequent searches.

A typical pitch has two features: a narrative or story about the job highlighting those aspects the headhunter believes will tempt the prospect, and a question designed to test the prospect's interest in the job. Narratives are presentations in which headhunters create an idealized portrait of the job along with an equally flattering picture of the person likely to be selected for it. As Rich put it, "When I'm recruiting, I don't call up and say, 'Hey, are you interested in a job?' I paint a picture, a mental picture or a quick picture of the position that I have available to try and whet this person's appetite." A typical presentation combines specific nuggets of information about the position with fairly generic descriptions of what qualities candidates for the position should possess. The nuggets are the bait for attracting a wide range of candidates. A headhunter's primary concern during the initial stages of a search is to ensure that any candidate who might possibly be qualified does not get overlooked; the narrowing of the list to the top candidates occurs later. Further, unqualified or mismatched candidates are not wasted because they can be added to a headhunter's database and become part of his network.

The following presentations are typical narratives. The first is one given by Gordon, an RSC recruiter who specializes in low-paid store manager positions. Over the past two months he had placed fifteen store managers with Regis, and he now claimed to have an exclusive relationship with the company. Gordon explained that Regis wants "attractive young women" for these positions, which pay less than $20,000 a year. His recruiting strategy was to call managers of other stores in the mall in which the Regis store was located to see whether they could recommend anyone to him; in this instance he was calling stores in the Brookfield Mall in Milwaukee. His script barely varied as he went from one store manager to the next, each call lasting about five minutes. He began by asking for the store manager. When she (all were women) picked up the phone, he explained the purpose of the call and introduced himself: "I need one minute of your time; this is a who-do-you-know call. I'm a recruiter based in [Southern City]." This was followed by a brief description of his client and the opportunity: "My client is Regis, a $1 million company based in Minneapolis, very upscale. They're expanding from 180 to 2,000

stores. This thing is taking off. They're looking for a store manager."
This was followed by a brief description of the qualities Regis sought
in its store managers: "They emphasize personality over experience.
They're looking for someone with a high energy level." If requested,
Gordon would tell the manager the position's salary, and he normally
concluded by asking if he could leave his name and number in case
she thought of someone she could recommend.

This pitch was clearly one Gordon felt comfortable delivering,
judging by how little he altered it over the course of the calls. In fact,
at one point he joked that the calls were putting him to sleep. Tightly
worded scripts, as other researchers have discovered, can be very re-
assuring and even empowering for salespeople in the uncertain world
in which they work (e.g., Leidner 1993). Asking for help, which is
how Gordon opened the conversation, is a common feature of sales
calls (see Oakes 1990). Many headhunters use this ploy to get the re-
cipients of their calls to cooperate, as Brian noted when reviewing his
presentation for us:

> Well, first off, what I always say, William, I have a sort of a
> spiel I go through. First off, I identify myself. I tell them, "I'm
> Brian J., I'm a recruiter. And the reason I'm calling, I was won-
> dering if you could help me." Ninety-nine percent of the people
> want to be able to help somebody. And I begin to tell them
> what I'm looking for: "I'm looking for this, somebody with this
> kind of a background. Blah, blah, blah. Do you know of any-
> body that would have some interest?"

His respondents, he added, generally tried to be helpful: "Most people
are very, very nice. Occasionally you'll get somebody that's rude. But
not very often."

Asking for help actually serves two purposes. First, it provides a
justification for the call and for the recipient to talk or, or at least listen to, the caller. Second, it is an indirect way of finding out whether
the recipient himself is interested in the job. Headhunters recognize
that to ask someone outright whether he wants the job is often ineffective because it makes the prospect wary and defensive. By starting
with a seemingly innocuous statement such as "I need your advice"
or "I need your help," a headhunter can get a prospect to relax his
guard; the conversation can then be steered toward the prospect's
qualifications and aspirations. Scott, the insurance recruiter, de-

scribed how he accomplished the transition from asking for help to prospecting by "softening up" prospects:

> I call them up and say, "Look, I'm an insurance recruiter, been working in the business for a long time, I'm currently working on a position, and would like to pass it in front of you if you have the time now, and just see if you may be able to point me in a direction." Now that's a very unobtrusive, "Oh, you want my advice." Now guaranteed in the back of my mind I know I want this person, and then you start getting personal after you tell them the job, and they say, "Let me think about it" or whatever. You say, "Well, just for my records, do you mind if I ask you a few questions? How long have you been with the Travelers?" You soften them up beforehand and then it's not, "I want your résumé, and I want you to change jobs for me right now." Because that's basically what we're doing, but with that soft sell it allows us to meet, to get away from the used-car mentality."

The second presentation is one given by Les, an experienced recruiter at BR (he had worked there more than five years). Les was trying to find candidates for a position with the Guinness Brewing Company handling sales and distribution in Louisiana, Alabama, Arkansas, and Mississippi. In his conversations with prospects Les attempted to hook them with his depiction of the Guinness managerial culture. Guinness, he suggested, was a company divided into "Indians" and "chiefs." The Indians were the "old-line beer people," and the chiefs were the "young, aggressive, consumer-products people." The problem the company was facing was that "they have too many Indians; they need more chiefs." Some of their consumer-products managers had left the company recently, and it was now short on "bench strength." Les's presentation was intended to suggest that the prospect not only had the right characteristics (young, aggressive, and consumer-products oriented) but also would be part of the group that would shape the company's future (the chiefs). Flattering candidates is one of the most noticeable features of these presentations. A headhunter says a candidate has been "highly recommended" when in fact she found his name in a company directory. Jobs are frequently described as requiring an "unusual" combination of skills or a "very unique individual."

None of the headhunters we observed or interviewed was a practitioner of the hard sell. For example, when Les identified and spoke to someone he considered a particularly promising prospect for the Guinness position, he could tell the response was noncommittal. He then suggested an "informal" meeting—"not a formal interview, just sit down and get to know each other"—between the prospect and a division manager at the company but could not get him to agree to this either. Les concluded the call after the prospect said he would think about the informal meeting. If a prospect does not commit to going on a job interview, headhunters often propose an "exchange of information" meeting with the client, which they are careful to emphasize is not an interview. If a prospect refuses any kind of meeting, the headhunter steers the conversation to those jobs or organizations or locations the prospect might like. Rather than attempt to persuade her to take a job she has said she doesn't want, the headhunter tries to learn what jobs are on her wish list and what makes them so attractive. For example, after it became clear to Dawn that one of her engineering prospects was not interested in the position she was pitching, she backed off: "We're not trying to drag you out of there now. That's not what we're trying to do. I don't know you, and you don't know me." Then she flipped the conversation to his preferences: "So location would be on top of your wish list?" In this way she learned that he wanted to remain in Texas, along the Gulf Coast, and that his wife's career was also a factor (she was a psychotherapist). Finding out what jobs are on a prospect's wish list has another advantage: it gives the headhunter an excuse to contact the prospect in the future. A conversation can be concluded with the statement, "So if this kind of position [i.e., a position that a candidate has just said he would really like to have] became available, you would like me to call you?" Few prospects are likely to say no to this. Doug claimed he wouldn't even pitch a job on the first interview, preferring instead to use this call to learn a prospect's "wants and desires."

Even if a prospect is interested in the job that is being pitched, a headhunter offers her the chance to withdraw from consideration. Marcie concluded a call to one of her candidates by declaring, "In closing, Anita, let me establish something with you. If at any point in the process you decide this isn't the right opportunity for you, don't think I'm at all interested in pushing you. I'm on your side!"

Of course, a headhunter cannot really be on the candidate's side because the candidate is not her client. Nevertheless, in watching and listening to headhunters talk to and about candidates, we were struck by the extent to which they did *not* view their interactions as "contests of will," to use Robin Leidner's (1993) phrase. Leidner has argued that insurance agents intentionally define their relationships with prospects as adversarial in order to ascribe a more manly, heroic quality to their work. Indeed, seller-customer relations are often highly competitive, as others have noted (e.g., Partnoy 1997), and headhunters themselves are often opportunistic toward clients. Candidates, however, appear to elicit from headhunters some of the "service idiom" that Guy Oakes (1990) has suggested coexists with the "commercial idiom" in sales work. (Effective sales personnel, he argues, are those who are untroubled by these contradictory idioms and are able to ignore the paradoxes they generate.) Our explanation for the headhunters' soft-sell approach to prospective candidates is their realization that leaning heavily on a prospect will make him less rather than more likely to go on the job market. Further, because candidates must ultimately sell themselves, headhunters need candidates to want to go to a job interview rather than to be browbeaten into going.

Qualifying Candidates

When a headhunter qualifies a candidate for a position, she wants to know whether he has the necessary skills to do the job, whether he is movable from his current job, and whether he is compatible with her client. If any of these factors is a problem, she will probably not present the candidate to her client; instead, he will become an entry in her database.

Identifying a candidate's skills is relatively straightforward. A phone conversation is usually sufficient for a headhunter to learn where the candidate went to school, what his major was, what his first job was, what his subsequent positions have been, and what he is doing currently. Headhunters focus most of their attention on candidates' most recent employment and probe these jobs at some length. For someone in a sales position, the questions hone in on accounts handled and products launched. For an engineer, the questions address the projects on which he has worked and the processes with which he is familiar. For a logistics position, the questions are about which computer programs the candidate knows. Candidates are also asked how many people they supervise and what their job titles are. And a headhunter may establish a candidate's track record by asking him what he considers his major achievements. Headhunters test lower-level candidates, such as legal-support workers and office staff, to assess their knowledge of legal terminology and their word-processing skills. All this information serves two purposes: it indicates whether the prospect is capable of performing the job, and it enables the headhunter to present the candidate effectively, to brag about him to her client, as one headhunter put it.

As important as a candidate's skills is his movability. A headhunter knows that if a candidate will not change employers, his qualifications are of little use to her client. There are a variety of reasons why a candidate may decline an offer. Fear of change, particularly for long-time employees, is always a possibility. A counteroffer may prove too tempting. Personal factors, such as the feelings and wishes of the other members of the family, are likely to complicate the decision, especially if the job change requires a geographical move.

Headhunters attempt to assess the risk of a turndown by continually testing the candidate's commitment to accepting the new job. For example, Gene identified two factors he used to determine movability. The first was whether the candidate was willing to go on a job interview without delay—within the next twenty-four to forty-eight hours, if necessary. The second was whether the candidate was willing to start work within two weeks of accepting a job offer. Anyone who failed either of these tests was not ready to cut her ties to her old employer, and Gene would hesitate to present her to a client. Another strategy is for the headhunter to gather as much information as possible about the candidate's family. Consequently, headhunters routinely ask candidates questions about their marital status, spouses' employment, and children. For example, when Jenny found a prospect at Macy's for Luria's LP/audit position (the "auditor from hell" search), she first questioned him about his work background and then shifted gears: "Let me ask you some silly questions. Do you have your driver's license? Are you a U.S. citizen? Do you own your own home? For how long? Are you married? Does your wife work?" She was pleased with all his answers because she observed, after she hung up, "He's good, his wife doesn't have a real job [she was self-employed], and he's owned his home long enough to make a profit."

Headhunters acknowledge that these questions are intrusive and, in some cases, illegal. Henry explained:

> We'll call a candidate up and they'll be interested in the job and we go, "Great!" Now's when the qualifying starts. A lot of companies stop at that point and send a résumé or set up an interview. We don't. That's when we get started. We get into some things that quite frankly a lot of people tell me we shouldn't get into. But I get into them. And a lot of candidates say, "You don't any have any business asking me these questions." I'll say, "Then I'm not sending you into the company." But I get into things like spouse's employment: "What does your spouse do?"
>
> "It's none of your business."
>
> "Oh yeah it is. . . . If you've got a daughter who's the head cheerleader next year, and she's a junior in high school about to be a senior, I want you to go talk to her before we go any further. Make sure that she's going to move."

One headhunter said he had on occasion called a candidate at home, at a time when he knew the man wasn't there, just to make sure his wife was aware of the job opportunity and was willing to relocate.

For any headhunter, however, the most difficult part of qualifying a candidate is determining whether she and the client are compatible. Headhunters insist that all hiring decisions are founded on the chemistry that is created between candidate and client during the job interview; chemistry, they argue, forges the attachment required for the job to be offered and accepted. They liken this process to courtship and marriage, with themselves as matchmakers. Headhunters accept that chemistry is to a certain extent unpredictable and, therefore, uncontrollable. As Henry said, "You put them together, make sure that it's a match, and then they either fall in love or they don't fall in love." Nonetheless, headhunters attempt to engineer the chemistry by finding out as much as they can about their candidates' personalities and backgrounds, by learning about the cultures of their clients and the preferences of the hiring managers, and by coaching candidates for their job interviews. In the next two chapters we examine how headhunters determine client preferences and how they coach candidates; in the remainder of this chapter we identify how they assess candidates.

Headhunters learn about candidates by questioning them on the telephone, examining their résumés, interviewing them in person, and checking their references. All headhunters call candidates on the phone and scrutinize their résumés, but for practical reasons, only headhunters who work the local labor market normally meet their candidates. They use these meetings to appraise their candidates' personalities, appearance, and self-presentations and to gather evidence about their nonverbal communication. Forrest explained: "There's a lot of questions that you have trouble asking over a telephone that become self-evident face to face. Whether somebody makes eye contact when you're talking to them. Whether there's a spontaneous response in response to things that you're saying." Headhunters with far-flung candidates and clients have to rely instead on experience, intuition, and reference checks to decide whether their candidates have the right chemistry.

Reference checks allow a headhunter to get a third party's perspective on the candidate. For these checks to be effective, however, headhunters have to do them creatively. One strategy is not to use the term *reference check*, in order to avoid having the call transferred to human resources, where the caller may receive little more than the dates of employment. A headhunter contacts a reference and says that his name has been given to her by a candidate who said "you'd be willing to share with us some insight into the way he thinks and works." This line, as Forrest pointed out, gives the reference no way out: it implies that the candidate has trusted the reference to reveal information about him—although it has not been called a reference check—so by refusing to talk or by switching the call to HR, the reference is casting doubt on the candidate's judgment. A second strategy is to find and call references additional to those the candidate has recommended. Headhunters often say they want references from people in three categories: a candidate's superiors, a candidate's peers, and a candidate's subordinates. Candidates typically provide the names of superiors only, but, headhunters point out, bosses often have a limited view of the candidate's performance and abilities. Peers may provide more accurate and reliable data about a person's capabilities, and subordinates can tell the headhunter how he treats others. By combining information from all three sources, a headhunter hopes to develop a sense of what the candidate is really like and whether he will fit well with her client.

No matter how well qualified a candidate, however, a headhunter has achieved little until she has persuaded him to become a real candidate, that is, to go on the job interview and be willing to accept the offer should it be made. Headhunters persuade candidates to cross this threshold by finding their "wounds."

Finding the Wounds

Good candidates meet two basic criteria. First, they are qualified for the position. Second, they are successful and contented employees—but not so content that they cannot be persuaded to consider a fresh opportunity. The ideal candidates are employees who are content without necessarily being completely happy; the headhunter's task is to identify the job or company where they can be both successful and happy. In contrast, employees who are looking for other jobs are less desirable because of the suspicion that their eagerness to leave their current employers is due to their being second-tier performers.

Headhunters assume that every job, no matter how good or desirable, is less than perfect. There is always at least one dimension on which it fails to satisfy its occupant entirely; this dimension is the employee's wound, or "hot button." A headhunter's skill lies in identifying and accentuating the impediment to an employee's complete satisfaction, in "finding and pounding the wound," as Scott put it. Headhunters suggest that jobs have five aspects that are potential wounds: the type of company an employee is working for, the type of boss she has, the responsibilities and duties of her job and how they advance her career, the geographic location of the job, and the salary. From a headhunter's perspective, the least-preferred wound is an employee's salary. The problem with money as a wound is that it is too easily healed with a counteroffer. An employee who feels she is underpaid and who becomes a candidate in order to raise her salary will, if she receives an acceptable offer and is valued by her current employer, almost certainly receive an equal if not better counteroffer. As much as a headhunter may caution a candidate about the "danger" of accepting a counteroffer (see chapter 8), if money is the sole wound, she is very likely to accept it. For the employer it is cheaper to keep a good employee by paying her more than to find a replacement, and for the employee the security of a familiar working environment at an acceptable salary is more desirable than starting afresh somewhere new. Headhunters argue that as the labor market has tightened, employers have become increasingly likely to use the counteroffer as a retention tool.

If an employee states that money is her reason for considering a job change, a headhunter either drops her as a prospect or seeks another wound. Ben said: "You have to find something in the makeup of the person that's a hot button other than financial. You've got to dig and find out what don't they like; it's got to be something. . . . So find out what that is, dig into it, push, push, push, push, push, and every time you talk to them, just go back and reiterate to them, 'This is really what you don't like, this is really what you don't like.'" Locating and pounding wounds serves two other purposes for headhunters. First, it tells them how to present the job to the prospect: once a headhunter knows what a prospect wants, he can sell the job in terms of how it meets those needs. Second, it begins the process of "closing" the candidate on an offer, whether in the present or in the future. Headhunters favor a closing technique that Robert Prus (1989b) calls "closing by inquiry," in which, having located the prospect's wounds, they ask him some variant of the following question: "If I found you a job that addressed this need or needs [the wounds], and assuming the money was right, you would be willing to seriously consider it?" If the prospect still hesitates to commit, it lets the headhunter know she does not have a candidate. But, headhunters say, if they have identified the wounds correctly and found a job that appears to salve them, they expect the prospect to become a candidate—to go on the job interview if requested to do so.

It is through discovering these wounds, therefore, that headhunters attempt to acquire the psychological upper hand in their production of job candidates. Ray described the process as "trying to break them down so that they trust me to tell me what they're really thinking." By knowing what a prospect was thinking when the opportunity was first presented to her, a headhunter can remind her of all the reasons she was considering a job change. In the absence of any formal control over prospects, headhunters rely on being able to irritate the wounds to turn prospects into candidates.

In their recruitment of candidates headhunters enjoy far less leverage than they have over clients; consequently, it is not surprising to find that recruitment is the area where headhunters are most likely to be deceptive. Whether they are engaged in identifying candidates, pitching job opportunities, qualifying candidates, or locating wounds, headhunters are seldom fully truthful. Indeed, it is hard to imagine how they could be effective without deception. Headhunters succeed by manipulating prospects' and candidates' fears, vanities, and weaknesses; these are the tools that enable them to take charge of a relationship in which they are ostensibly the weaker party.

6

Finding the Right Person for the Job

Specs, Hot Buttons, and Chemistry

> Every, every, every placement is a chemistry placement. And
> don't let anybody tell you any different, okay.
>
> —Gail, A Southern City headhunter

For more than two decades, academic analyses of employee selection
and promotion have advanced the view that the employees who get
ahead are those who "fit" the best with their superiors. Renowned organizational scholars such as Rosabeth Moss Kanter, Jeffrey Pfeffer,
and Robert Jackall have all made the argument that getting ahead by
getting along is a common feature of corporate life; indeed, it becomes more common the higher the level in the organization.

Fit refers to an employer's sense of comfort with and trust in an
employee. The importance of this factor in hiring and promotion decisions is now widely acknowledged. Rynes and Gerhart (1990) note
that their study of applicant fit was prompted by the frequency with
which company recruiters explained their employee-selection decisions in terms of fit. Pfeffer states that "the idea of 'fit' is mentioned
extraordinarily frequently" by corporate recruiters and job applicants
(1989, 386). Jennifer Chatman writes that employee selection appears
to be based in large part on criteria such as "personal chemistry, values, and personality traits" (1991, 461).

Fit is the product of two related factors: social similarity (Kanter
1993) and social skills (Jackall 1988). Social similarity refers to
whether members of organizations are part of the same social networks, that is, whether they share class and ethnic backgrounds and
have similar social experiences. Kanter argues that the greater the uncertainty associated with a position and, therefore, the greater the

personal discretion required of the incumbent, the more likely it is that incumbents will be selected on the basis of social similarity (1977, 54). Social skills refer to a person's ability to manage his external appearance, to mask his emotions and intentions, and to display a personal style that puts others at their ease and indicates he is a person of good taste and judgment. Jackall argues that the higher a manager rises in the organization, the more difficult it becomes for his superiors to assess his performance and competence and the more his continued advancement depends on his mastery of social skills (1988, 39–59).

This brief discussion of fit raises a number of interesting issues. First, both Kanter and Jackall assert that fit matters most for upper-level positions because these are the ones in which trust and evaluation are the most uncertain. Remove uncertainty, they claim, and the need for fit will decline correspondingly. Second, Kanter and Jackall suggest that assessments of fit are in effect synonymous with assessments of the likelihood that a candidate can "do the job." In short, fit is skill. This line of argument implies that skills and previous experiences that cannot be reduced to social similarity or style play only a minor role in the selection of new employees. Third, the different levels at which fit operates have not always been clearly distinguished. Some researchers suggests that fit is a relationship between an individual and an organization. This conceptualization looks at the extent to which job candidates match up with the employing organization's strategies, values, norms, and culture (e.g., Rynes and Gerhart 1990; Chatman 1991), what we call candidate-organization fit. Others see fit as involving a relationship between individuals, such as between a hiring manager and a job candidate (Bills 1988; Jackall 1988; Kanter 1993), what we call candidate-interviewer fit. Fourth, Kanter has pointed out that when social similarity determines who gets hired or promoted, those who are different—primarily women but also men from a less-favored social or ethnic background—are severely disadvantaged. The use of fit as a selection criterion results in discrimination.

The Headhunter Theory of Employee Selection

The activities of headhunters are guided by a theory of employee selection that involves specs, hot buttons, and chemistry. Even poorly defined positions tend to have at least rudimentary specs. Specs include, most typically, a description of the position, a list of requirements regarding education and experience, and the anticipated salary. For example, the specs for a search for an engineer might be three to five years' experience in machine design in a high-volume manufacturing environment, supervisory experience, a degree in mechanical engineering, and a starting salary of $55,000.

Headhunters claim that although specs help determine the composition of the pool of viable candidates, they fail to provide enough information to guide the selection of one candidate over another when two or more candidates meet the specs. "They tell me nothing," was one headhunter's curt assessment of the specs just cited. Given the conviction that "there are a number of qualified people for most positions," headhunters suggest that specs are best understood as a *negative* aspect of selection because they help determine who will not be chosen. Job offers, they argue, hinge on an employer's assessment of two *positive* and often unstated selection criteria: hot buttons and chemistry. Headhunters believe these criteria are the keys to the hiring decision: it is how effectively candidates meet these criteria that determines who will land the job, once the preliminary screening based on the formal requirements has been conducted. As Larry put it, "A monkey can understand the specs . . . but where you lose placements is on the qualitative, on the intangible." Identifying the intangible or unstated criteria is, therefore, crucial.

Hot Buttons

Hot buttons are highly specific skills and experiences to which a given employer reacts favorably. Unlike specs, hot buttons are not baseline experiences or skills expected of all viable candidates; rather, they are talents or skills that give a particular employer reason to become sufficiently enthusiastic about a particular candidate to extend an offer. One headhunter usefully defined hot buttons as the "solution to the problem that motivated the employer to seek to fill the position." Another defined them in terms of skills and experiences that would meet an employer's "dire need."

Hot buttons need not be particularly complicated or nuanced. For example, the hot buttons for the engineering position just mentioned turned out to be successful experience in designing jigs and fixtures and performing vendor quality audits. In some cases a hot button can be a higher level of education than is stated in the specs. For example, when Walter got the order for the five loss-prevention managers at Office Depot (see chapter 4), he immediately scrawled "NO GUMSHOES" across the job-order form. He knew, even though it was not stated in the specs, that Office Depot expected its loss-prevention personnel to be college graduates, not traditional store detectives. In other cases the hot button may be a previous employer. RSC headhunters know that if they are looking for a store manager for Pic-n-Pay shoes, they need to find someone from a rack-shoe retailer (so called because all their shoes are displayed on racks) rather than from a high-end retailer who stocks shoes in the back room. Ben knows that Coca-Cola Foods is most pleased by candidates with prior experience at General Foods or Procter and Gamble, although that is not stated in the specs, because of the quality of managerial training at these two companies. Hot buttons are often context specific. They vary widely over time and across positions, departments, and companies for even the most narrowly defined occupational specialties.

Sometimes hot buttons depend more on the hiring manager than on the job or organization. Headhunters claim that certain hiring managers look for particular types of experiences and skills in *all* the candidates they interview, making hot buttons specific to the hiring manager rather than the position. An illustration of this kind of case emerged during our fieldwork at RSC. Walter was trying to find a director of taxation for Office Depot. Although this assignment might appear to be a fairly straightforward search for someone with an accounting or finance background, Walter knew there were two other unstated requirements. First, the successful candidate would have to be a CPA because both the chief financial officer and the vice president for finance, the officers who would make the hiring decision and to whom the position's occupant would report, were CPAs. Second, Walter knew the company was looking for someone who had the capacity to do long-term strategic thinking—they were searching for an "intellectual."

Hot buttons mean that skills matter in the hiring decision. Kanter and Jackall seem to have overlooked the important and independent role played by skill in the selection process. Headhunters use general credentials and experience (the specs) to guide their initial screening of candidates. To become viable, however, candidates must satisfy headhunters that they also possess at least some of the idiosyncratic qualifications and experiences—known to headhunters but not to candidates—that are required of the new hire. Hot buttons serve as markers of a candidate's ability to do *the* job, not just *a* job of the sort being filled. A successful candidate, however, must also show that he or she fits well with the client, that there is the requisite "chemistry" in the match between candidate and client.

Chemistry

Chemistry (sometimes referred to as *personality*) denotes an employer's highly subjective evaluation of the quality and ease of interaction with a candidate. Many headhunters spoke of chemistry in terms of rapport, the sense that one can understand another and be understood without undue effort. In this sense, chemistry is very close to what Jackall described as the "easy predictable familiarity that comes from sharing taken-for-granted frameworks about how the world works," a familiarity that makes others "feel comfortable"(1988, 56). Chemistry is based on the compatibility between the candidate and the hiring organization's culture, norms, and strategies; it is also based on an interpersonal compatibility between the candidate and the hiring manager.

Communicative ease is not the sole way in which headhunters understand chemistry. Headhunters also spoke of chemistry in terms of positive affect, an idea more vividly expressed in a phrase headhunters often use: "People hire people they like." Jeff, an industry trainer and headhunter, expressed a commonly held understanding of the way affect—either strongly positive or strongly negative—could sway a hiring decision.

> I have seen placements where the person couldn't do the job, but he or she was such a nice person that they said, "We are going to hire this person. We like them." But I have *never* [spoken with considerable emphasis] heard anybody say, "This person is dead on for this job. This person is perfect for this job. But she is a jerk. We are going to hire her." The reverse never works. If they don't like them, they don't hire them. If they like them, they will make allowances in other areas.

Chemistry operates at two basic levels. The first level implies that organizations have particular cultures, norms, or strategies with which candidates must mesh (e.g., Rynes and Gerhart 1990; Chatman 1991). Chemistry at this level refers to candidate-organization compatibility. Consider first the idea that someone who might be qualified to perform a given line of work might fit well with one organization but badly with another. For example, Larry described the specs for one of his current job orders as consisting of two years of experience as a general manager of a Houston's or a TGI Friday's restaurant (or some other restaurant with at least a million dollars in sales). Candidates with that background may nonetheless be unsuitable in the employer's eyes because they do not fit the organizational culture:

> The owner of some restaurants that we will go to, man they drill, they're like drill sergeants, and that's what they want. They want someone who's going to whip these waitresses and waiters into shape, and come hell or high water, it's my way or the highway. These other restaurants, you know, hey, we want to be happy and be fun. We do this and we do that, and when someone makes a mistake, we want to retrain them. Well, you send that military guy to that kind of company, well, this guy's way off base. Well, what do you mean? He's got the specs. It's not going to work.

Here candidate-organization fit depends on what might be called managerial orientation. Owners appear to be the main decision makers in the restaurants with which this headhunter works; in those workplaces new hires must fit the owner's preferred managerial orientation.

Headhunters suggest that a second level at which chemistry operates may be at least as important in the selection process as candidate-organization compatibility. They believe the candidate must develop good chemistry with the person or persons conducting the interview and making the hiring decision in order to have any chance of being selected. Fit at this candidate-interviewer level has two main components. The first centers on the personality traits of the interviewers, especially the hiring manager. Similar personalities are thought to enhance candidate-interviewer chemistry, as Ted explained:

> We're trying to find a personality match. If I have a very nebbish character [a hiring manager], he's very introverted and I'm dealing with a guy [a potential candidate] who's very extroverted on the other side, well, that's not going to work. Why waste my time even if he's qualified. . . . Likes hire likes. So

much for diversity. Likes hire likes. That's reality. But I try to
get somebody who has similar features, similar background,
similar personality as the person who's interviewing them.
That's the ideal goal if you can do it.

This statement is especially important in light of the fact that it was
made by a headhunter who places highly technical computer specialists whose "personalities" would not appear to be directly related to
effective performance on the job. Nonetheless, "nebbishness" is a
trait that enhances fit, and hence employability, in this particular
company with this particular hiring manager.

The second component of fit at the candidate-interviewer level involves a variety of background experiences and current traits and interests that help a candidate establish and maintain rapport with the
interviewers and the hiring manager. These traits are more strongly
connected to social similarity than they are to personality, although
there is some overlap between the two. Headhunters like Ben inter-
rogate their candidates for evidence of the kinds of non-work-related
characteristics they believe will generate good candidate-interviewer
chemistry:

> I'm looking at what you do on the weekends, family, do you
> play golf, do you play tennis, do you like to read? Try to find
> out as much as I can because people hire people just like them-
> selves. That is an absolute truth in this business. If you sit
> across from me and your background is very similar to my
> background, we kind of had the same things growing up, I'm
> going to gravitate to you faster than I'm going to gravitate to
> some guy who lived in Boston all his life or New York, or
> Philadelphia, or San Francisco. It's just people hire themselves;
> they love to do it.

It is important to underscore here the same point we made about personality traits. Namely, headhunters are emphatic in saying that attributes and experiences that enhance a candidate's likelihood of establishing good chemistry with one organization and hiring manager
might represent neutral traits or even chemistry killers at a different
organization or with a different hiring manager.

Virtually every headhunter we spoke to or observed stressed the
critical importance of chemistry. For example, Jeff claimed, "I've

found that 80 percent of every hire is chemistry, regardless of the technical specs." Sam, who specializes in the construction industry, put the estimate somewhat lower: "Let's face it, out of a placement, if you were to break it down to 100 percent of it, the technical side of it represents 50 percent. Once you get that, the rest is personality." Most headhunters spoke of chemistry in more general terms, suggesting that it is the key to hiring decisions. Gail's description of the role of chemistry is typical:

> Every, every, every placement is a chemistry placement. And
> don't let anybody ever tell you any different, okay. You can put
> three people or four people in front of somebody, and they're
> going to hire the one that they have that rapport with, all other
> things being equal. If they're all qualified—they all have the
> degrees, the background, the skill level that they're looking
> for—they're going to go with the one that they feel the best
> about; and that's chemistry. And that's the thing that's the cru-
> cial element.

In fact, many headhunters claim that good chemistry overcomes weaknesses on a résumé. Gene declared: "Once you get chemistry rolling, it can overcome paper [i.e., a résumé] very easily." The reason is simple: "No one hires paper."

One of the implications of the salience of chemistry is that headhunters present candidates who lack all the required qualifications, who are considered, in headhunting parlance, to be "light." In fact, experienced headhunters often suggest it is futile to search for the "perfect candidate" because a headhunter's definition of perfection is not necessarily the same as the client's. For the client, it is the uncertain and idiosyncratic factor of chemistry that determines which candidate is perfect. Gene, therefore, uses what he calls the "60 percent rule": candidates are presented to a client provided they have at least 60 percent of the qualifications, including the essential ones, for which the client is looking. He recounted an experience at UPS, where he had filled a position with a "dynamite" candidate who lacked a college degree, even though a degree was a stated requirement. Other candidates had the degree, but the chemistry between them and the hiring manager was lacking.

The skill in presenting candidates is to find the right balance between being too tough in evaluating prospects, or searching for perfection, and being too lenient, or not being sufficiently discriminating (what headhunters refer to disparagingly as "throwing résumés against the wall and hoping that one sticks"). It is not easy to achieve this balance; Gene's 60 percent rule is more a gut evaluation of a candidate than a true quantification of his or her skills. Headhunters have to make sure they do not miss the critical hot buttons. Brian provided an example from a current search. He was looking for a plant manager, with the main requirement being that candidates had successfully transformed a unionized plant into a TQM facility. He would not present candidates who claimed they could do it unless they actually had the track record: "My client needs somebody that's done it." One of the easiest ways for a headhunter to lose his good reputation is to send poor-quality candidates to a client. Candidates may be light, but they should not be weak.

Light candidates in fact serve two purposes for headhunters. First, there is always the possibility that they will be hired. Second, they can be presented first, before the strong candidates, thereby "framing" or accentuating the qualities of the strong candidates as well as providing a way for headhunters to learn more about the client, the hiring manager, and the interview process for the benefit of subsequent candidates. In the next section we discuss in greater detail how headhunters use first candidates to gather information of this nature.

Our results confirm that previous studies (e.g., Jackall 1988; Kanter 1993) were not wrong in suggesting that fit plays an enormous role in the selection of new employees (even if these studies have underestimated the importance of hot-button skills). In fact, we would go further than Jackall and Kanter in two respects. First, fit is critical to the recruitment and hiring of all white-collar employees, not just managers. Second, it is a selection criterion that is still very much in use, many years after the introduction of various "diversity" initiatives aimed at increasing the social and cultural heterogeneity of workplaces. Although Kanter's afterword to the second edition of *Men and Women of the Corporation* suggests that workplaces are moving "from homogeneity to diversity" and that "the managerial priority" has shifted to "managing and even affirming diversity" (1993, 290), it is worth reiterating what Ted said about the continuing role of fit in employee selection: "Likes hire likes. So much for diversity." In short, social similarity remains more consequential than Kanter's recent statements imply.

Discovering and Constructing Hot Buttons and Chemistry

Hot Buttons

Headhunters grasp and shape hot buttons through a complex blend of activities. Some of these activities are designed simply to gather information, to discover the hot buttons; others represent an effort to exert an influence, to collaborate in constructing the hot buttons. Some of these activities are visible to employers; others entail a form of clandestine detective work. As they attempt to match candidates to clients, headhunters strive to obtain unusually rich, position-specific information on selection criteria. They seek such information because they believe their ability to "control the process," to engage successfully in what academics call third-party impression management, depends on their understanding of hot buttons and chemistry.

Hot buttons are either discovered or constructed. Some employers understand and readily divulge to a headhunter a position's hot buttons on their own. In this case headhunters need simply to confirm their understanding of the hot buttons. For example, Frank recounted a client who sought to launch a new consumer product in the health and beauty field. The client knew and announced at the outset of the search that it wanted "someone who's had new product introduction, who has been with this type of organization, who's had a successful, documented track record." If the hot buttons are not immediately apparent or if the client is new, headhunters ask probing questions, as Ben described:

> When I'm working with a brand new manager I've never worked with, I don't have an established relationship so I'm not going to know what the hot buttons are for that person. So what I'll do is say, "Listen, I understand what your company, Johnson & Johnson, wants. I understand the profile. Tell me about you, what are you looking for?" . . . What I do is I make up a profile. I say, Bill Smith with Johnson & Johnson has, this is what his hot buttons are, so anybody I send to him I need to make sure that they're prepared to either show examples or deal with this when he turns around and asks it.

This headhunter went on to say that Bill Smith's hot buttons for prospective candidates included how they managed people, accounts, and discretionary funds; how they developed new business and the careers of their subordinates; and what kinds of computer systems they knew.

Probing questions are directed at the hiring manager, not human resources. As we saw in chapter 3, though headhunters accept that they have to deal with HR, they exert every effort to bypass that department and speak directly to the hiring manager when they need to learn what the hot buttons are. Doug explained:

> Meade will send you very lengthy job descriptions, and she [an HR staffer] has in every case here. What I found, though, and maybe it's just on my part, that they are very boring. What I find is it's better for me to talk to the hiring authority and say, "Look, what are the three or four most important things to you in evaluating whether this person's going to be right?" You find out what are the nuances as far as terminology for the job, and then you focus on, "Okay, what's really important to you?"

Job descriptions—the specs—are not credible indicators of what is sought in candidates, nor do those descriptions, or HR staff members, help headhunters establish which selection criteria have the highest priority. Headhunters believe the HR staff is too far removed from the job and the hiring manager to understand the hot buttons and chemistry required of a new hire.

On other occasions headhunters discover hot buttons through trial and error—by literally making mistakes. Kevin told us that early in his career he was asked by a bank to find a vice president of construction lending. At the time he had no idea what the function of this position actually was, but by asking around he learned it involved financing the development of small office buildings for medical practices and other professional groups. He began to recruit and found what he thought was an outstanding candidate: "He was an MBA from Duke, he had three years' worth of experience, I met him, I mean he looked like he came off of GQ." He set up the interview and afterward called his client to learn how it had gone. He discovered to his dismay that his client wanted candidates to have had direct experience in financing construction deals; his candidate lacked such experience. The headhunter recalled the embarrassment of the post-interview conversation with the client, but he used the information provided to recruit an acceptable candidate:

> This guy [the client] ate me for lunch. He explained to me that this guy [the candidate] was a trainee, he had done no deals. . . . And I mean the guy [the client] ran me through the wringer, and I listened to every word he said to me and all of a sudden I realized that the MBA wasn't important, that the style wasn't important, that what it was somebody who could do the deals, who had familiarity with these kinds of transactions, who had done dah, dah, dah. And I renumbered my priorities, I went back, and you know what, I found the guy.

In many cases, however, hot buttons are not buried in the specs or even known to the hiring manager: they must be constructed through a dialogue between headhunter and client. Bernie, a headhunter and trainer who places industrial engineers, described how he helped a client form the hot buttons that would guide the selection of a new hire. He called this strategy the upcoming-project approach:

> Well, many times they haven't thought enough to answer my questions about what is it they want me to find. So you have to help them. I had an engineering manager. He wanted an industrial engineer with five years' high-speed manufacturing experience. I said, "Let me ask you this question. Are there any projects coming up that this person might affect or work on in your company?" "Well, yeah, Bernie, we're going to redo our plant layout next year." I said, "Okay. Since you have that major project coming up, wouldn't it be good if I find you somebody with good experience in plant layout?" And he says, "Yeah, that'd be good." Okay. Now I understand the key to the hire.

The hot button in this case, experience in plant layout, was formed by getting the client to consider upcoming projects. In other cases headhunters prod the hiring manager to describe in some detail what the position is likely to require of a person during a typical day. Like the upcoming-project approach, this walk-me-through-a-day approach helps headhunters bring definition to the job description and the selection criteria. Yet another approach is to ask the client what outcomes are expected from the occupant of the position, which is a way of "working backwards" to the hot buttons, as Randy explained: "You tell me what outcome you're expecting, and we'll go backwards. We'll find people who can produce that outcome." By getting clients to think harder about organizational objectives, headhunters believe they acquire a clearer sense of clients' hot buttons.

All three approaches conclude in the same way: the headhunter describes his understanding of the hot buttons that will guide the selection decision. If the hiring manager agrees with the headhunter, the collaborative act of constructing the hot buttons is brought to a close. A disagreement prompts additional discussion of the position and the selection criteria.

There is a deeper way in which hot buttons can be socially constructed. In some cases hot buttons are not fully discovered or constructed until the client begins to interview candidates. Headhunters suggest that there is often a notable difference between a client's pre-interview claims about hot buttons and what emerges once a few interviews have been conducted. Karen addressed this issue:

> A company can give you this grandiose description of what they're looking for. Then you send a candidate out there, and you find out much more from the candidate as far as what they're looking for. A candidate really helps you fine-tune what the client company is looking for. Sometimes I don't think they know, and I think maybe a candidate is either a great fit or not a great fit. And they kind of define the position based on who comes in there. They say, "This is what we don't want because this candidate fell short." Or, "This is what we do want because we like this."

Like others, this headhunter uses her client's "grandiose," pre-interview statements about hot buttons as a starting point—as criteria that guide the selection and presentation of a first candidate. In the language of headhunting, that first candidate serves in part to "test the job order," to determine the degree of divergence between the abstract representation of selection criteria and the concrete evaluation of a flesh-and-blood candidate. A consequence of this strategy is that first candidates are seldom the strongest candidates, at least in the headhunter's eyes. They are unsuspecting information receptacles that headhunters will drain of data in the post-interview conversation and use for the benefit of subsequent candidates. As Ben explained, once he had identified the three main questions the first candidate was asked, he could tell subsequent candidates, "Here's your three areas you need to be focusing on; these are his hot buttons."

Early candidates, however, are more than mere test cases who help a headhunter clarify a client's hot buttons. Headhunters argue that such candidates often serve to redefine hot buttons and other selection criteria because of the specific skills and experiences they either do or do not possess. Clients can see something in a candidate—positive or negative—that comes to play a central role in defining what is and what is not sought in the new hire. Hot buttons are thus best understood as discovered and constructed through an evolving sequence of interactions.

Once interviews begin, headhunters acquire information both directly and indirectly. Headhunters can and do discuss directly with clients the merits and demerits of early candidates in order to further refine their understanding of hot buttons and chemistry. But they can also obtain a wealth of information from candidates by debriefing them after the interview. Put simply, candidates are routinely pressed to provide a form of client reconnaissance. In the following excerpt Jeff role-played a debriefing call to explain how he conducts such conversations and what he attempts to learn:

> "Sue, how did it go?"
>
> "It went pretty well. I met Norm. I was there for two hours. We talked about the job. I think it is something that I might want to pursue. He said he would call me back."
>
> We've got to dissect this. First of all, I say, "Great, Sue! Let's get more specific. Now that you have seen the job, you know more about it than I do. You give me your version of what that job actually is." You want to ask her the same questions you ask the company.
>
> I say, "Let me tell you right now that companies hire solutions to short-term problems. What do they seem really concerned or anxious about?" The answer to that is the key to the job order, usually.
>
> I also ask, "Now that you have seen it, can you do the job?" If she says, "Yes, I think I can," ask, "Why? How does it relate to your experience?" Make them tell you why.

Then ask, "What questions were asked? How was the interview structured, Sue? What did he actually ask you? Who else
did you talk to?"

In another example from our fieldwork, Marcie, a headhunter at
Technology Services Associates, debriefed a candidate, Jill, after her
interview at Georgia-Pacific (GP). Notice how Marcie finds out from
Jill what the two hot-button questions are:

Marcie makes a call to Jill, in California: "Jill, are you awake?
Remember—you're the one who told me to call so early!" She
says she wants to know how Jill's interview with GP has gone:
"I wanted to touch base with you before I heard from GP." She
listens for about two minutes while Jill talks, then notes, ap-
provingly, that Jill appears to have developed good rapport with
Blake, one of the two interviewers: "Good, good. That's a positive. From what I know, you'd be parallel with Blake. It would
be important for you to be in sync with him." As she talks,
Marcie types items into Jill's database record. She begins to
probe: "What was that last question he asked you? Remember
that one? We both had the sense that it was prepared—right?
Wasn't it, 'If the project was . . . ' How did it go?" She listens
and types, then comments: "So that's it! Good. Was there
something else?" Apparently, there was another question that
Marcie finds noteworthy because, after listening to Jill's response, she asks: "What does that mean?" She listens and types
some more, then cracks a joke: "Did you tell him that you'd
jump out of the thirty-eighth-floor window!" I can hear Jill
laughing at this.
Marcie is pleased with how Jill has handled the interview:
"That's important. You sound like you did a good job of reading
those individuals." On her screen Marcie has now typed in the
two questions in which she was interested: "How would you
feel about presenting a schedule that slipped?" and "How
would you handle external-internal schedules?"

The first question refers to how a candidate would react if a project
ran over schedule, which is a common occurrence at GP. The second
question gets at how a candidate would coordinate the mix of con-
tractors, vendors, and regular employees who make up GP's payroll;

this mix requires someone in the position for which Jill is being considered to make tough decisions about who does what. These questions came up at the end of Jill's interview, and Marcie believes they are GP's hot-button questions for the position, which is why it is so important that she know them. The questions go into Jill's record and also into the new record Marcie is creating about Roger, the other person at GP who interviewed Jill. In this way other headhunters will have a sense of his interviewing approach before they send candidates to him.

The headhunters to whom we spoke all debrief candidates after an interview. The examples just described focus on the details of the job and show how candidates are another source of information that allows headhunters to understand better the screening practices of a client company and the selection criteria that are likely to guide the hiring decision. Other debriefing calls focus more on the perceived chemistry between the client and the candidate. The purpose of the debriefing call, therefore, is to obtain additional information that can be squared with what is gathered directly from the client, both before and after interviews begin. In this way headhunters can develop insights into hot buttons and chemistry that do not depend directly on the client's willingness or ability to share information.

Headhunters work to discover and, if necessary, construct hot buttons because well-defined hot buttons are critical to finding good candidates and making placements. When a client fails to disclose or collaborate in the construction of hot buttons, headhunters feel that they are unlikely to make the placement and consequently give that particular search short shrift. As George commented, "I'm just basically throwing résumés out there—and we tend not to do that." In contrast, well-defined hot buttons provide the ammunition for the headhunter to make a powerful candidate presentation to the client.

A good illustration of the connection between hot buttons and candidate presentations was provided by Bernie, who delivered and contrasted two presentations during his explanation of the importance of hot buttons. The first is what he called a generic presentation based solely on the position's specs.

"Hello, Joe, this is Bernie over at ABC Search. You gave me
that job order for the industrial engineer. I want you to know
that I've got three five-year industrial engineers that have been
working in high-speed manufacturing environments just like

yours. Now the one that I like is a B.S.I.E. out of Georgia Tech, and he's looking to make a job change. I felt you might want to see him for that position you have."

The second—and much preferred—presentation is based on the plant layout hot button identified in an earlier discussion with the hiring manager:

"Joe, it's Bernie over at ABC Search. You put me on a search for that industrial engineer. I've come down to three that I thought were good for you. You may want to see all three of them. But one stood head and shoulders above any engineer I talked to for this reason: not only does he have the five years you want and a B.S.I.E. out of Georgia Tech, but he just redesigned the plant layout for his present company. The results were 22 percent more product output based on his design. We're talking three quarters of a million dollars in gross revenues for his company. I felt certain that's the man you want heading up that project you have coming up. What are your thoughts?"

Notice how this headhunter incorporates the hot button into a common sales technique: the feature-benefit presentation (Weitz, Castleberry, and Tanner 1995). Headhunters believe powerful presentations based on hot buttons give employers reason to arrange interviews and to act decisively in making strong offers, as opposed to low-ball or lateral ones. Information on hot buttons is thus translated by the headhunter into a kind of sales leverage over clients. It is also key to a headhunter's ability to prepare candidates for interviews (see chapter 7).

Chemistry

As with clients' hot buttons, headhunters learn about their chemistry predilections in various ways. In many cases they are familiar with a client's background and personality from having worked with the client before. Lisa explained:

We know our clients pretty well, and we've worked for most of them for a while now. And we know what they want. We know what they are looking for. . . . So we put personalities together. We put, you know, some law firms are very laid-back firms. If it's an entertainment law firm, you're going to have some pretty interesting characters, not only who work there but certainly as clients as well. It's a whole different style than working at one of the top ten firms in the city. It's a lot less stuffy. A lot less corporate.

If the client is new, a visit is a good way of gathering information, as Gail pointed out: "It is important to sit across the desk from a client to find out exactly what they need, getting a feel for the corporate culture. You know, what kind of atmosphere? How do they dress? How do they talk? How do they look? Is it a plush environment or a functional environment? I mean, is it mahogany row or is it steel-case desks?" Gail has the advantage that all her clients are local. A headhunter with far-flung clients has to spend time on the phone getting to know them. Regardless of whether headhunters meet their clients in person, they use their initial conversation to ask probing questions: "Tell me about yourself, Mr. or Ms. Controller. Where did you go to school, how long have you been at this company, where were you before? Why is the incumbent that you're firing or who quit, why was that person successful or not?" They are also asked about the company culture, as George noted:

> The first thing I do when you give me a job order, I go over the culture, you tell me what you want, you tell me what you don't like: "Hey, I don't like Auburn grads or I hate people from Florida or whatever." Whatever your little quirks are, right? And I'll get the company culture, what do you like: "Well, we don't like people that are cocky, we don't like people that are not aggressive, or we don't like people that are not CPAs and we would prefer an MBA, we don't care about whatever." Everybody's got their little quirks. We take that and we'll go to our database and we'll pull out people.

Early interviews are also an invaluable source of information about chemistry. Headhunters use client and candidate feedback from these interviews to try to get the chemistry right. The lessons learned from an interview by an unsuccessful candidate are often crucial; Michelle described a typical conversation with a client:

> If they [the client] say, "Well, we just didn't care for her," I ask, "Was it skills or personality?"

[Client:] "Well, personality. I think she's a little too quiet."
[Headhunter:] "But did you feel the skills were right?" Because you want to know if you were close and then, "But you're telling me that a too quiet personality is not going to fit into that group, right?"

Headhunters discover chemistry and make placements on the ruins of unsuccessful interviews, as Brian explained: "Feedback from my client is what gets me going more than anything else. Even if it's bad feedback, even if they tell me this candidate you sent us does not have just what we're looking for, that's okay. At least I can tailor my search efforts to what they need."

Discrimination, Diversity, and Chemistry

The considerable effort headhunters put into discovering or constructing hot buttons is powerful evidence that the recruitment and hiring of new employees is not simply a matter of chemistry. Skill, independent of chemistry, is clearly a vital element in the selection process, and it would be a mistake to assume that if experience and skill requirements are hidden or unstated, they are nonexistent. Nonetheless, headhunters acknowledge, hot buttons can be overshadowed by chemistry because it is this factor that ultimately determines who gets the job, especially in situations in which two or more candidates can press the requisite hot buttons. Thus headhunters concentrate their efforts on finding candidates who not only meet the specs and can push the client's hot buttons but also possess something in common, in terms of background or personality, with the client. Headhunters are guided by a simple conviction: "Likes hire likes."

A conviction of that sort raises the possibility that headhunters are deeply involved in perpetuating patterns of inequality in the labor market. Given the continued overrepresentation of white men in positions that wield hiring authority (Reskin and Padavic 1994; Jacobs 1995), it is natural to assume that social and demographic outsiders are not evaluated fairly or presented as candidates if headhunters are indeed convinced that "likes hire likes." It is possible that hiring managers direct headhunters to restrict their searches in blatantly discriminatory ways; it is also possible that headhunters infer that clients have discriminatory preferences and then use those assumed preferences to guide the identification, evaluation, and presentation of candidates. Such actions would be instances of overt discrimination on the part of headhunters. More subtle forms of discrimination might involve practices that serve to perpetuate patterns of inequality even though they do not stem from or involve a deliberate or conscious desire to discriminate. So-called image requirements for certain positions and organizations can be gendered and racialized (e.g., Sokoloff 1980; Kennelly 1999) and thus act as barriers to women and racial minorities.

Headhunters revealed and discussed selection criteria relevant to assessments of fit that were discriminatory and sometimes illegal. By far the most common discriminatory criteria mentioned by headhunters were age and appearance. Gender and race also emerged as salient—though not always negative—factors in the evaluation of candidates and the assessment of likely fit.

Age and Appearance

Headhunters believe clients want candidates of both sexes who are young and good-looking. By and large, headhunters avoid older candidates, as the following conversation between two TSA headhunters reveals. Jonathan was trying to explain to Louis why a candidate, Wade, was unsuitable for a position as a programmer. He remarked that he thought Wade lacked some of the necessary skills and then added, "And he's older—he's over fifty" (Wade was fifty-three). After further discussion of Wade's qualifications, Jonathan asked Louis if he was going to call Wade. Louis said he was, to which Jonathan retorted: "Wait until you talk with him." Jonathan explained that Wade sounded even older than his actual age on the phone: "I'd say he sounds at least sixty-five on the phone." Louis laughed at this and then observed that an "old voice" can kill a person during a phone interview.

Appearance is often mentioned as a knockout factor as well. Concerns about appearance tended to be a mixture of two ingredients— beauty and weight—with an occasional reference to physical disability. Many headhunters described the importance of organization- and job-specific notions of appropriate beauty. This concern was especially pronounced among those who worked the clerical and support-staff market, where candidates had to have the "right look" for front-office work. In our fieldwork we observed an interaction between

Gail and Pat, who Gail thought might be a suitable candidate for a job as assistant to the director at the national headquarters of a paralegal training school. Gail emphasized to Pat that the job would require a certain look: "This is [X], you know, the premier address in [Southern City]. That means daytime makeup, hair up not down, and suits or nice dresses." Appearance in this and other cases was not simply a matter of proper grooming and attire: candidates had to be physically attractive. Part of being physically attractive is the subjective notion of acceptable weight. In this connection Larry combined weight and physical disability in a single statement: "What's a TGI Friday's looking for? I guess, no, we don't discriminate, but I mean they're not going to hire someone that's four hundred pounds, you know, and walks with a limp."

Headhunters claim that clients are unlikely to state explicitly their preferences regarding age and appearance; they have to be inferred, as Ben pointed out:

> My companies don't openly come out and say, "Don't send me someone like you." I mean, they'd have no interest in looking at a forty-two-year-old, receding-hairline, five-foot four-inch guy. I'm not saying they openly discriminate, but if it came down to a twenty-eight-year-old walking in the door or me, the twenty-eight-year-old is going to get the job nineteen out of twenty times. And these companies that I work for don't openly say, "I will not look at this person." But they often find reasons to knock the candidate out.

Suggestive statements of this sort are common. Headhunters often need to interpret ambiguous or deliberately misleading feedback about candidates from clients. In doing so, they may rightly or wrongly conclude that discriminatory criteria guide the evaluation of candidates.

Age and appearance are most likely to come into play when headhunters unearth marginal candidates—those who may be able to press some but not all of the hot buttons—or when two or more candidates cover the relevant hot buttons. It is in these cases that headhunters may well decide not to present candidates who are too old or are, as one exclaimed, "like me—short and dumpy." On other occasions a headhunter will pass the responsibility for rejecting an unprepossessing candidate to the client, as Ben explained:

If they [a candidate] come in and they're five foot five inches tall and 175 pounds, I will go to the employer and say, "I have met this person, and this is what they look like." And I know the employer's going to knock him out, but at least that's not me playing God. I let them do it. And I've got to gently go back to the candidate and say, "There's now an internal candidate who has surfaced that they're looking at strongly."

This headhunter is well aware that candidates who are too old or who are physically unattractive or overweight will simply generate no chemistry with hiring managers for the types of sales jobs he fills. Though he claims he does not "play God," he cloaks the client's selection criteria by telling his candidate that an internal candidate has knocked him out. In that way Ben and other headhunters permit and perpetuate a client's discriminatory practices.

Gender and Race

Although many headhunters mentioned the importance of age and appearance during our interviews and fieldwork, we uncovered few direct and negative references to links between gender and race and assessments of candidate fit. Race and gender surfaced most often in discussions of what headhunters called "diversity searches." Headhunters claimed many of their clients would explicitly state that they wanted a "diversity candidate," which tended to be defined in racial and ethnic terms rather than gender, in order to boost counts of such employees. As Ben put it, "It's a numbers thing. There aren't many [minority candidates] out there. Their [an employer's] EEOC counts are down. That's where the search will be." Significantly, this and similar comments offered by headhunters suggest that corporate demand for white-collar minorities stems more from external pressure, a point emphasized in Sharon Collins's (1997) analysis of the black middle class, than from the "affirmation of diversity," as suggested by Kanter (1993, 290). External pressure may subvert the explicit use of gender and race as proxies for likely fit.

Headhunters themselves are well aware of the EEOC pressures faced by employers. They may take advantage of these pressures to market minority candidates as MPCs (most placeable candidates). For example, at Lincoln Search we listened as a headhunter marketed a minority female to a Southern City construction firm. Before making the call, he explained that he had found an ideal MPC. She was a thirty-something project manager with a B.S. in civil engineering from Purdue University. Most important, she was African-American and female, a "two-fer" in headhunter-speak. The opening words of his phone conversation made it immediately apparent that he was framing her in terms of her ascribed characteristics, which he believed would grab his respondent's attention: "Once in a while you come across someone you want to market. It's a project manager—she's black, female, very polished, highly articulate, quite advanced in her career, her salary is in the mid-fifties." The fact that she was African-American was interpreted as money in the bank, not a knockout factor.

Few headhunters described situations in which a candidate's race or gender overtly served to clinch or undermine fit. One subtle link between these ascriptive criteria and fit involved image requirements for certain positions and organizations. For example, many headhunters spoke of the highly "athletic" character of some hiring managers and work groups, and how older and overweight candidates would be unlikely to fit well with such people and contexts. Settings of this sort, although ostensibly gender-neutral, may in fact result in gender bias by leading headhunters to favor men, who on average are more likely than women to participate in and be involved spectators of a wide range of athletic endeavors. Consider also Ben's claim that a successful candidate for the sales positions he fills must have a "commanding presence." In practice, that meant successful candidates tended to stand about six feet two inches tall, weigh about 175 pounds, and have dark hair and blue eyes. Although gender, race, and ethnicity did not surface explicitly in his discussion of image, tall, blue-eyed candidates are more likely than not to be white men, not women or people of color.

Two headhunters described more obvious cases of bias that became evident over time as clients reacted to candidate interviews. Kevin, who specialized in positions involving the analysis or marketing of financial products or their services, described at some length the way a candidate's gender played a role in his dealings with Japanese banks in Southern City, which are structured as agency offices able to make loans:

> As backward as we may be in our dealings with women and minorities, we are light-years ahead of the Japanese. Women in Japanese society are seen as detail-oriented individuals. You

will find no women in positions of major prominence in government or business or anything in Japanese society. So for the Japanese to operate in this country and the way that we do business, they have had to make some major concessions from a societal perspective. But for me to say to a woman that "this is a great job for you" is not up front. That no matter what, they are going to be overcoming a societal difference in the way that people who have been socialized in their pre-adult life have come into the U.S. now are being told that you know all those things that you felt about women—forget about it, they're peers. They're going to be doing marketing just like you. Well, that isn't necessarily so.

It is important to emphasize that Kevin did not say or imply that he would not present women as candidates to those organizations. It is clear, however, that he did not feel he could credibly sell the job to female candidates as an attractive opportunity. As we described in the last chapter, most commonly a headhunter must pitch a position with enthusiasm if he is to have any chance of enticing a well-placed and rewarded prospect into becoming a candidate for the job. If Kevin cannot say "this is a great job for you" to a woman, it is unlikely he will have any female candidates to present to the client.

These same organizations appeared to prefer whites to blacks as well. Kevin continued:

In this area where we have a significant minority population, much of which is highly trained and educated, much of which are very talented people. To say to an individual that you're going to be readily accepted from a society which is basically entirely of the same segment, that you're going to be accepted in there, is wrong. So I add that not only in terms of what the integrity is that I have to say to a recruit but also what the reality is that I'm going to make the placement. Because if I'm a Japanese selecting officer and I've got a white candidate from one recruiter and a black candidate from another, guess which one is going to get hired? So those are the realities of the things that you have to deal with, and those are the things that I have to say to people about the realities of an opportunity.

Two aspects of Kevin's statement merit comment. First, his understanding is that blacks, like women, will encounter prejudice if not discrimination in this organization. We doubt, however, that Kevin had a full and frank discussion about these patterns of discrimination with potential candidates, despite his allusion to "things I have to say to people about the realities of an opportunity." Rather, we suspect he maintained his "integrity" by refusing to pitch the job to blacks as a good opportunity—to, in effect, fail to woo rather than repel. Second, he goes beyond his statements about gender by suggesting, though not directly stating, that black candidates will not be hired. In the place-or-perish world of headhunting, there are strong incentives to identify and present viable candidates, thus perpetuating, rather than challenging, a client's discriminatory selection criteria.

In a second case Eric, who filled management positions in the wireless communications industry, described the candidate he presented in a recent search for a vice president for human resources. The candidate was rejected by the client in large part because she was a woman:

> I got what I thought was the magic bullet, and everything started happening: they talked, the guy flew to Chicago to meet her, loved her, she went out to Seattle and spent a day and a half. . . . But when she went in and talked to these people, 50 percent of the people didn't want her to leave the building. I mean they said, Don't even let her out of here, we need her, she's perfect. Twenty-five percent of the people said, Well, I see some problems, she's so young; but her background is so good and she knows so much, we should hire her anyhow. But the other 25 percent were totally turned off because she is a very aggressive female. She's a senior vice president at a telecommunications company in Chicago who has taken a company from 89 employees to 3,200, very talented. And a female to make that kind of jump in a company in six years, I mean she stands toe to toe with the guys.
>
> Well, engineers are not necessarily the types that like strong females. And again this is broad, but the typical engineer's wife brings his slippers and his hot chocolate every night to him. Where the senior staff guy, the VP type guy of marketing or general management, usually has a strong wife behind him.

They're used to strong women; nobody up there had problems with this girl, but the engineering guys—and this is an engineering company, it's a software company—they thought they couldn't work with her. And it was mostly because she's just direct and straightforward, and in this company she worked for, I mean it's an engineering company as well, but yet these engineers didn't like the way she came off with them. Because she was so aggressive and so straightforward and, "This isn't so hard; we just do it, guys." I mean that kind of attitude and they didn't like it and the company was unwilling to piss off a couple of engineers; they wouldn't hire her. She was just, I mean, this woman was one of the best people in the world, I mean from a recruiting standpoint I did the right thing. I had the right person, and now we're starting all over again.

So that's the way they are; they won't hire unless it's perfect. It has to be exactly right; everybody has to be on board before they'll hire. And not every company's like that. A lot of companies will look at the good, look at the bad; we've got a balance here, and if that balance looks pretty good, we're going to go ahead and do it. They're not that way; it has to be just perfect.

Eric expressed considerable frustration at having to "start all over again" on what had already been a long and difficult search. It was clear that he felt he had indeed uncovered the "magic bullet," the perfect candidate for the job; it was equally clear that he had learned a lesson, namely, that this particular company, replete with what he understood to be gender-traditional male engineers, would not hire a woman for this position. The client's reaction to his female candidate would surely deter Eric from presenting another female candidate for this position. Significantly, however, Eric did not appear to generalize that gender bias, and he stated here and elsewhere in the interview that other companies behave differently. The fact that Eric presented a female candidate in the first place and then believed she was the magic bullet is evidence that he did not enter the search with the conviction that gender would be a knockout factor.

In sum, our analysis of evidence regarding age, appearance, race, and gender revealed three main patterns. First, we identified several cases in which a headhunter *inferred* a client's taste for discrimination on the basis of image requirements or a client's history of rejecting particular types of candidates. Inferences of this sort may, of course, be correct or incorrect, but in either case they are likely to be consequential in imposing limits on the headhunter's identification and presentation of candidates. Second, our evidence suggests that headhunters are unlikely to position themselves as strong advocates of nondiscriminatory selection criteria. The twin imperatives of pleasing clients and making placements mean that headhunters have strong incentives to permit and perpetuate a client's tendency to devalue older workers, females, minorities, and those who are overweight or unattractive. Third, although some headhunters suggested that age and appearance were key, though unstated, selection criteria, few mentioned or implied that race or gender played a similar role. There seems little doubt that race and gender are two among a number of factors that influence social similarity, but our interviews and observational evidence did not suggest that assessments of chemistry—or candidate evaluations more generally—were routinely dominated by a candidate's race or gender.

It is possible that we simply failed to uncover the extent to which race and gender shaped the evaluations and actions of headhunters. For example, it is reasonable to argue that the litigious climate surrounding the hiring of women and minorities made headhunters unwilling to discuss or reveal how race and gender operate to ensure—or kill—chemistry. Headhunters, like employers, can be sued for discrimination in hiring. We doubt that we overlooked the explicit use of gender and race in assessments of chemistry, however, in part because we did, in fact, observe and hear about the blatantly illegal use of age as a selection criterion. In addition, methodological research on face-to-face interviews suggests that male respondents (the bulk of our sample) are most likely to express inegalitarian and even discriminatory views about gender inequality in employment when interviewed by men (Kane and Macaulay 1993), a characteristic of all the evidence collected for this study. Similarly, the fact that we are both white would have encouraged our mainly white respondents to be more forthright about the salience of race as a selection criterion than if either of us was a member of a minority group.

It is important to recognize that one form of unintended discrimination may be part and parcel of the headhunting trade. As we described in the last chapter, a headhunter strives to identify prospects brimming with accomplishments and accolades; she then works to turn those prospects into candidates for one or more positions she is hoping to fill. Individuals who are relatively less visible in organizations, less senior, and less recognized and rewarded may simply not appear on a headhunter's radar screen. To the extent that gender, race, and ethnicity shape the processes whereby workers rise to the top in organizations, it is reasonable to conclude that the candidate identification and selection process used by headhunters perpetuates patterns of inequality.

Implications for Workplace Diversity
Our findings have two rather somber implications for workplace diversity. First, some scholars appear to us to be too optimistic about the possibility of achieving diversity in the workplace. For example, Kanter (1993) has argued that managers' desire for socially similar others in the workplace—what she calls "homosocial reproduction"—reflects the amount of uncertainty in organizational roles. Similar arguments have been made by Jackall (1988) and Pfeffer (1989). Uncertainty, according to Kanter, increases reliance on trust and personal discretion and leads to the selection of workers on the basis of social similarity. If uncertainty can be reduced, greater diversity in hiring can be expected.

Our evidence, however, does not support Kanter's hypothesis that the desire for socially similar candidates varies substantially across different types of white-collar jobs or over a wide range of employers. With the exception of a few cases in which an employer was desperate to hire someone with uncommon technical skills, virtually no Southern City headhunter even hinted at the possibility that there were hiring situations in which candidate-interviewer fit was not critical—if not *the* key—to the selection decision. The explanation for the persistence of chemistry in the evaluation of job candidates may well lie in the social psychology of trust and evaluation. Researchers studying group processes have found that people are predisposed to evaluate socially similar others in positive terms. They are also likely to attribute negative or undesirable behaviors among social similars to external causes rather than individual faults. Finally, they are usually unaware of their in-group bias (Kramer, Brewer, and Hanna 1996; see also Baron and Pfeffer 1994; Lin, Dobbins, and Farh 1992; Rand and Wexley 1975). Our sense is that these processes are difficult to alter and hence serve to undermine efforts to diversify workplaces.

Second, other researchers have reported that formal or "open" recruiting methods—a category that is defined to include recruiting through advertisements and employment agencies—minimizes the use of ascriptive criteria in hiring (Reskin, McBrier, and Kmec 1999; Reskin and McBrier 2000). Our results suggest, however, that headhunters clearly use ascriptive criteria in selecting candidates (even if such criteria do not always include the most notorious ones of race and gender). Headhunters, after all, strongly believe social similarities are key to selection decisions, and they perpetuate the tendency, usually associated with informal hiring methods, for likes to hire likes. From the headhunter's point of view, the ideal search assignment is one in which she quickly and effortlessly identifies and presents a single candidate who is a dead ringer for the hiring manager. The workaday world of contingency headhunting, however, is far from that ideal, and headhunters often end up presenting candidates who lack some of the desired experiences and skills and/or fall short of being socially similar to the hiring manager. In practice, then, headhunters do not present *only* socially similar candidates to employers. Their theory of employer selection decisions, however, leads them to work toward that end, *possibly even in situations in which social similarity might not be a selection criterion*. In those situations a headhunter's theory of selection would entrench the use of social similarity as a selection criterion and make headhunters another mechanism in the homosocial reproduction of labor.

7

Fitting the Right Person to the Job

The Dynamics of Third-Party Impression Management

It's just that everything in life is presentation. And if something is presented more favorably, people feel better about buying it.

—Michelle, A Southern City headhunter

A considerable body of recent scholarship, much of it based on experimental research, has suggested that interviewer assessments of the competence, ability, and fit of job candidates are "subjectively created realities influenced in large part by the active efforts of the actor [the job candidate] toward the observer [the interviewer]" (Gilmore and Ferris 1989, 196; see also Kacmar, Delery, and Ferris 1992; Ferris et al. 1991). This process is known as "impression management" (Rosenfeld, Giacalone, and Riordan 1995; Giacalone and Rosenfeld 1989). In this chapter we take the analysis of impression management from the laboratory to a "real-world" setting by examining how headhunters attempt to manage the impressions clients and candidates form of each other.

Third-party impression management has received scant attention from researchers, whether experimentalist or nonexperimentalist, even though there are various allusions to the actual and potential role of third-party impression managers in some of the classical statements on group dynamics. For example, Simmel's (1950) analysis of the *tertius gaudens* suggests that a third party can smooth over the troubled interactions of the other two parties. Goffman's *Presentation of Self in Everyday Life* (1959), a theoretical cornerstone of the impression-management literature, contained a chapter on "teams" that explored the management of impressions through the coordinated activities of two or more individuals.

The neglect of third-party impression management is striking also in light of recent developments in the impression-management literature. Kacmar, Delery, and Ferris summarized the focus of an emerging line of research when they argued that "the particular characteristics of the situation or context, and the behavior that is situationally defined as appropriate, will contribute to the success or failure of different impression management tactics" (1992, 1254). The "situational appropriateness" of a candidate's behavior—what Roy Baumeister (1982) has termed "audience-specific" self-presentation—determines how the candidate will be perceived and whether various impression-management strategies will be effective. The problem of situational appropriateness arises because interviewers vary widely in how they respond to a candidate's behavior and statements (e.g., Bretz, Rynes, and Gerhart 1993; Mayfield and Carlson 1966) and because candidates don't know what would be best for them to do or say in different contexts (e.g., Liden and Parsons 1989; Fletcher 1989). Without context-specific information, candidates risk engaging in situationally inappropriate behavior—in having their impression-management efforts inadvertently produce false negative evaluations (Fletcher 1989).

Every job candidate faces the challenge of providing a summary autobiographical account of her strengths, background, and skills in response to the following type of question: "Tell me about your background and especially about your experiences at AAA Corporation." This question is more difficult to answer than it may appear. The candidate first has to formulate mentally an account of her work experience. A complete, unabridged account of those experiences would be much too detailed and long-winded to serve as the text for a reply to the interviewer's question. Instead, she needs to begin a rather savage editing process to pare the account down to something compatible with the context of an interview. The candidate must select and delete material to produce a sample—perhaps random, perhaps not—of material from the complete account. She then needs to deliver that sample as the response to the autobiographical question.

The danger for any candidate is that her abridged autobiography does not contain the content the employer seeks in a new hire: it may be situationally inappropriate. A candidate may fail to show she has the right chemistry or fail to press the employer's hot buttons *even if the candidate's unabridged autobiography contains clear and convincing evidence that she has the right chemistry and can press the employer's hot buttons.* A form of sampling variability makes some truly worthy candidates appear less than fully desirable in the eyes of employers. Even the most honest and sincere job candidate can construct and deliver many different autobiographical accounts of her background, experiences, and skills. Some of those accounts pack more punch than others for a particular position with a particular employer; what is appropriate for one is not necessarily appropriate for another. The problem, however, is that most candidates get the opportunity to offer only one abridged account, and they may not select the one with the most punch.

A candidate would like to choose the situationally appropriate abridged autobiographical account—the one with the maximum appeal to the particular hiring manager conducting the interview—from the multiple accounts at her disposal. Her difficulty in selecting the right one is exacerbated by a lack of detailed information about the criteria by which the interviewer will evaluate the abridged, autobiographical account. In effect, job candidates are often in the position of having to make decisions about how to present themselves to what amounts to an unknown audience.

We argue that third parties, especially those well positioned and motivated to gather and share information and observations on an employer's hiring preferences, represent a *social* solution to the problem of situational appropriateness. By gathering information about clients' hot buttons and chemistry and then sharing it with candidates, headhunters greatly increase the probability that those candidates will provide situationally appropriate answers to client questions. Further, by sharing information with clients about candidates, headhunters make it more likely that clients will be predisposed to view these candidates positively. In short, headhunters engage in impression management of both parties in an effort to achieve what is for them the most desirable outcome: a match, that is, a job offer.

Direct Impression Management

Headhunters practice two forms of direct impression management. They handle potentially damaging, negative information about candidates, and they emphasize the recruited status of their candidates to attempt to persuade clients to treat them differently from other job seekers.

Defusing Negative Information

Information that points to a candidate's shortcomings is often more consequential than information attesting to his strengths because interviewers typically place more weight on negative information than on positive (Giacalone 1985). How headhunters respond to unfavorable information about candidates forms a large part of their efforts to manage their clients' impressions of their candidates. Although headhunters insist they always recruit excellent candidates, they admit they are frequently in the position of having to construct an image of a candidate in the face of evidence that is open to unflattering interpretations. They believe, however, that the information used to indicate performance quality, how this information is weighted and evaluated, and the overall assessment of performance quality are social constructions, not objective facts.

Headhunters use two main techniques to limit the impact of information that threatens to undermine the viability of someone they regard as an otherwise worthy candidate. The first involves informing the hiring manager in advance of the bad news and, in some cases, exaggerating it. Stan explained how exaggerating negatives could in fact help a candidate make a stronger first impression with a client:

> We can't stage the interview. But we can certainly prepare the person better, and we can prepare the client. So if the person is, we'll say, not visually attractive, that's politically correct but still discriminatory, or they have some mannerisms or twitch that isn't because of some medical problem, or if they have poor eye contact, or if they're refinishing their house and their hands look like a laborer's, we prepare a client for that. Sometimes we overprepare them so that the applicant even looks better: "You know, Stan, you prepared me for this guy who was coming. I thought he was going to come across badly. Well, you know, he's not that bad!" Well, some of that's technique to prepare them for the worst and have them be surprised.

This strategy can backfire if it dissuades the client from pursuing an interview with the candidate; it can also draw attention to an issue that might not have been noticed or defined as a problem by the hiring manager. Its advantage is that it leads the client to anticipate the worst; when the candidate turns out to be better than expected, the adverse information becomes far less consequential. Although risky, this tactic may enhance a candidate's viability in at least some situations. It also makes the headhunter appear to be a stern judge of candidates, a perception that can help boost her credibility and hence influence over the hiring manager. As Ray, a solo practitioner who places accountants and financial analysts, put it, "My philosophy is you're always selling credibility, nothing else."

A second strategy headhunters use for defusing negative information is to counter it with a plausible alternative interpretation that attempts to persuade the client that the damaging evidence about the candidate is only seemingly important rather than really important. Henry described how he would create a context to explain away a bad reference:

> I have had people with bad references that I've placed. Now they better have some good references, too. But I'll call the company up and say, "Okay, I've got five references on this guy. There's one that's bad. Here's what the first one says and here's why they say it and here are four good ones and here's why this whole thing takes place." And they'll hire the person. Somebody's got a vendetta or what have you. As long as I set it up. Now if I give them the references and they call them and hear that, it's death. They won't go any further with it. But if I set the plate right and let them hear why it happened and research it, then it works out.

More common than a bad reference, however, is a résumé that appears to indicate that the candidate lacks the skills and/or experience necessary to do the job. As we have shown, it is fairly common for a candidate to lack at least some of the requirements a client has specified in the job order, only to be evaluated by that client as being qualified. Nonetheless, a résumé that suggests a candidate is light in one or two critical areas may be an insurmountable obstacle unless the headhunter can convince the client either that the résumé is not a good indicator of the candidate's skills and experience or that these factors are not crucial to getting the job done. Rich recounted how he had talked a residential-construction client into interviewing a candidate whose résumé revealed no background in residential construction:

> Chambers Associates in Boston. Phil Chambers, the owner, needed a superintendent. Phil Chambers does commercial construction and residential construction. Sticks and bricks, we call it. And he told me that he was looking for a superintendent. In addition to commercial construction the candidate needed to have residential construction experience in his background. So by now I had learned a few things. I had a candidate coming in from New York. Arthur Lewis was his name. I had a résumé on Arthur and had interviewed him on the telephone and learned that his family from his early childhood were in the house construction business. He had most recently worked on a nuclear power plant and it was stated in his résumé—nuclear power plant for Stone and Webster. Concrete and steel and all that kind of stuff. Nowhere in the résumé did it say residential construction.
>
> I called up Phil Chambers and told him I had this candidate. See, here's the importance of marketing. I said, "I have a superintendent candidate who's coming into Boston tomorrow or in the next couple of days on his own for an interview, and he has residential construction experience. His family was in the business." Phil said, "Well, send me a copy of the résumé." I told him I didn't have a copy of his résumé. All I knew is that I recruited him and I've written down things I know he's capable of doing but I don't have a résumé right here in my hand. But I didn't want him to see it because he would have thrown it in the trash can. I set an appointment for Arthur Lewis. He went over, interviewed, and was hired. His most recent experience was working on a nuclear power plant; he hadn't done any residential in years. But once I got him in front of Phil Chambers, he had a chance to sell himself.
>
> So what I'm aiming for when I get a candidate and a hiring authority with some mutual interest, I want to get the two of them together physically and I'll have a better chance of closing that—that candidate will have a better chance of getting the position. You can't see everything in here, the résumé.

People write poor résumés sometimes, and sometimes they undersell themselves.

This case shows how a headhunter can counter the apparently negative information in the résumé by simply disputing its accuracy (and by refusing to share the résumé with the client). It is then up to the candidate to win the job by pressing the client's hot buttons during the interview. Even if a candidate is unable to press the hot buttons, a headhunter may still be able to get an interview and an offer by pointing out to the client that the candidate has other skills and looks like a good fit. Chemistry may override other weaknesses, as Ray noted in describing one of his placements:

> If they believe in me, if they think that I'm honest, I can influence somebody to consider a candidate that does not fit the specs. You'll talk to a client and say, "Look, I know this person." I'm thinking of a person I placed who had a Chicago MBA, undergraduate from Wellesley. Did she have any manufacturing finance experience—what they said they had to have? No. But man, she was about as sharp as they come. Excellent intangibles as far as interpersonal skills. Some related financial experience, but not really what they were looking for.
> And I called up my client and said, "I just spent two hours with this woman. She is awesome! She doesn't have what you're looking for, but I guarantee you if you talk to her, you're going to like her. You might not hire her, but you're going to like her and it's worth your time to talk to her." So they talked with her. Not only did she get a job, she got a good raise out of the deal.

The exaggerate-the-negative and plausible-alternative-explanation strategies are alike in that both are preemptive strikes intended to draw the sting from harmful information about a candidate before the client can use it to reject that candidate. They differ in that the former involves merely pointing out and possibly .exaggerating the negative information whereas the latter consists of challenging the meaning and salience of that negative information. These strategies are two of the ways headhunters try to put a positive "spin" on the candidates they present to clients. Direct impression management also includes headhunters' efforts to get clients to present themselves more favorably to candidates.

Getting Clients in a Selling Mode

One of the ironies of headhunting is that the best candidates are the most difficult to recruit (see chapter 5). The ideal candidate has a record of demonstrable success in his or her current position. That success usually means such candidates are well rewarded and secure in their jobs. Further, they are likely to have received many calls from headhunters eager to talk them into considering other jobs. As a result, they are cautious and even reluctant job seekers who are highly selective in what they deem a good opportunity. These characteristics present special problems for headhunters. For instance, a recruited candidate may well turn out to be what headhunters call a "window shopper," a candidate who rejects strong offers and enters the market mostly out of curiosity and, quite commonly, with an eye toward securing a counteroffer from his or her current employer. Even a candidate who is not a window shopper and who is receptive to the idea of a job change will be susceptible to the appeal of a strong counteroffer.

One of the ways headhunters attempt to convert contented employees into willing candidates is to find wounds, as we discussed in chapter 5. The headhunter's task is to locate the wounds and share this information with the client. The client, in turn, is expected to use the information in its sales pitch to candidates. Ben discussed how he translated wounds into selling points that a hiring manager could draw on by describing a typical conversation with a hiring manager:

> "They're [the candidate] with a boss who doesn't give them any autonomy, they're not allowed to have an expense account, they're not dealing with strong enough customers, and they're not feeling like they have control. Can you sell these things?" So I've already put in the back of the manager's head, here are my selling points. So what you're doing is you're targeting what the person's unhappy about with the manager so the manager will cover, here's what we'd like.

By getting clients to focus on candidates' wounds, headhunters are inverting the usual roles of buyer and seller held by, respectively, clients and candidates. These roles imply that candidates must persuade clients to buy their labor services; clients, for their part, can be quite selective, delaying an offer until they are fully convinced of a particular candidate's merits. Headhunters attempt to switch those roles by presenting recruited candidates as reluctant job seekers who are interested only in the *right* opportunity—not just *an* opportunity—because they have no need to make a job change. Headhunters emphasize to clients the need to recruit as well as evaluate and thus press them to sell the candidate on the position and the company. Headhunters call this process getting the client in a "selling mode."

Ray described how he tries to transform the general reluctance of recruited candidates to make a job change into leverage over the client: "If a guy's really, really happy where he's at but he's willing to listen to a better opportunity, you better be telling your client, 'Look, this guy was not looking for a job. I think the guy's great. But if you're going to get him, you're going to have to sell this opportunity. You're going to have to sell your company.' You really work on your client to be part of the recruiting process." He went on to explain how his activities as an information broker and go-between intensified if he was successful at getting his client in a selling mode: "And that's where a headhunter is really invaluable—if there's a mutual interest between the two people. Now you're talking to your candidate, saying, 'Look, I know you're really happy where you're at. How does this sound compared to where you're at? Well, what do they need to do?' And then that's the information I'm going back to my client with." Another part of getting clients in a selling mode concerns the kind of offer the client puts on the table to attract a recruited candidate. Since headhunters earn a fee based on a percentage of the new hire's starting salary, anything that helps produce an offer with a high salary directly benefits the headhunter as well as the candidate. As Chuck, a solo practitioner who places nurse and office staff in doctors' offices put it: "It serves my interests to do the best I can for them [candidates]. I say, I'm going to help me by helping you."

Headhunters thus strive to alter the expectations of both candidates and clients. The identification and wooing process produces recruited candidates who feel recognized and distinguished. Those perceptions will be amplified if the client adopts a selling mode. For their part, clients are led by headhunters to believe they have a top performer on the line who must be reeled in with care. A headhunter's objective is to make each party more attractive to the other as they approach the defining moment of the job interview.

Indirect Impression Management

The job interview is all-important because "no one hires paper." Impressive paper credentials, along with a headhunter's persuasive presentation of a candidate to a client, can secure an interview. Offers occur when a candidate performs well during the interview, generates good chemistry, and pushes the relevant hot buttons. The problem facing recruiters is that they are almost never present at that critical moment when client and candidate meet. The influence of headhunters thus reaches its nadir at a flash point. Headhunters cope with this problem through what they call "candidate prep." When headhunters prep candidates, they provide them with information and advice designed to shape and even alter the content and form of a candidate's presentation during the interview. Candidate prep is indirect third-party impression management because headhunters endeavor to create positive images of candidates by coaching them, as opposed to representing them directly in discussions with employers. The effects of coaching on evaluations, however, have received little sustained attention by students of employee selection despite some evidence that prepping can be quite influential (Sackett, Burris, and Ryan 1989).

General Prepping: Recruiters as Personal Trainers for Candidates
Prepping is divided into the general and the specific. (This analytic distinction is ours; it was neither mentioned nor used by headhunters.) General prepping typically involves advice about attire, conduct, and the content and tone of a candidate's oral presentation that headhunters believe will enhance the candidate's job prospects with a broad range of employers. These "dress-for-success" tips—get a new suit, make sure your shoes are shined, get a haircut, be clean shaven, mind your language and manners, offer a firm handshake, maintain eye contact—are the perfunctory but necessary steps any candidate must take. As Walter explained to one of his candidates, they don't get you the job, but they show "you're willing to play the game."

Much of the general prepping information is not specific to a particular interview. It is generic advice of the sort one could obtain from any book on job finding and interviewing. Where headhunters make a distinctive contribution is in tailoring their advice and feedback to the specific qualities and mannerisms of a candidate. Headhunters, in effect, act as personal trainers for candidates. Ben, for example, advises candidates about their clothes, despite the resistance he might get from candidates who feel that such coaching is unnecessary:

> I really spend a lot of time prepping, pampering, and babysitting my people. You could talk to anyone who's worked with me in the last ten years and they'll say, He's the biggest mother hen you've ever dealt with and I hated working with him, but he gets the job done.
>
> Q: Now what does that involve? What are some of the things you do?
>
> I prepare my candidate for what to expect during the meeting. That will be everything from "I know you're thirty years old and you've been with your company for eight years out of school. This company you're going to see is very conservative. Your hair needs to be short; you need to wear a dark blue suit, starched shirt, tie, shined shoes." They'll say, "You don't have to tell me how to dress!" But I do, because if I don't tell you how to dress, you might go in there with one of those wild paisley ties and this guy's going to go, "Oh, I loved him, but a little too wild for a first interview." And you've got to stay on top of the guy; tell him this is what you're going to wear.
>
> I've had people go in for the final interviews and they're traveling somewhere. I say, "How many suits are you bringing?" "I'm bringing one." "Bring two suits, two ties, two shirts." I had a guy four years ago sitting in a hotel lobby. Next door—he didn't know it—they were using one of these big balls, these demolition balls, and they slammed it into the building. The guy spilled his coffee all over himself. He had one suit. He turned around, went into the meeting. It was a 9 o'clock meeting—he wasn't going to get to go buy clothes anywhere. The client said to me, "We really liked the guy, but he should have been smart enough to have two suits." He didn't get the job because he had coffee stains all over him. I tell people, "Bring two suits for your meeting. I don't care if you don't want to carry an extra suit." I use that story.

Gail describes the advice she offers her office-support candidates who lack the kind of appearance and presentation that impress clients:

There are some that are extremely gifted in interviewing. But there are also the mousy little secretaries who come across like a worn-out dishrag, who are wimps, okay. They can't get hired because they do not present themselves well. So then it becomes a question of educating them. I have trained candidates in how to dress, what to wear. I have sent them to the makeup counter at Rich's. I have told them what kind of makeup to get, how to apply it. I've sent them to get haircuts. I've sent them to get nails done or put on. I've told them to take off the rouge and the makeup and just add a little bit because this company doesn't like it. I've told them to remove all jewelry and no perfume whatsoever. I mean, literally, you get down, when you're preparing a candidate, you tell them exactly what to do and how to do it in order to get the job. Because I know my client. They don't always hire the best candidates; they hire the candidates they like.

Headhunters' general prepping suggests two important points. First, headhunters are acutely aware that subtle—even trivial—differences between candidates result in one getting an offer while the other does not. There is no requirement that the perceived difference between the top-ranked candidate and the others be large. Minor elements in the way candidates present themselves thus take on an exaggerated importance and can make or break a person's candidacy. A truly odd and unpredictable combination of events—a demolition ball's impact, a full cup of coffee, and a lack of a spare suit—can become an indicator of a candidate's competence and character. Although headhunters recognize that they cannot foresee every danger capable of derailing a candidacy, they attempt to prepare candidates for a variety of contingencies. The two-suit tip is one example of what may appear to be a rather zealous effort to anticipate the unexpected and to have a suitable response for it. Second, headhunters believe a client's first impression of a candidate is critical in determining the candidate's viability, a point found in previous research studies as well (Dipboye and Gaugler 1993; Gilmore and Ferris 1989; Gladwell 2000). If the candidate does not make a good first impression, it is unlikely she will command enough of the client's attention to compete effectively with other candidates, regardless of her skills or previous experience. As Gail noted, "You only have one chance to make a first impression. If you walk in wrong, you won't walk in again."

Forrest provided another example of the importance of attire and conduct during an interview. As he points out, candidates are not professional interviewers and often do not know what will rule them out of consideration for a job. Headhunters, in contrast, hear horror stories of this nature all the time and can offer sound advice to candidates about avoiding mistakes that could cost them the job. Forrest said:

I've told candidates before, you need to change your shoes, you need to change your shirt, you need to shave your beard. You need to quit wearing that bracelet. I've told women you wear too much perfume. You need to not wear such a low-cut dress. All sorts of things. You've got to control the process that way. We had a situation six months ago where a woman didn't get an offer for a senior-level position, controller of a company, because she had on an ankle bracelet and a tattoo below her dress line. And those are things that candidates don't know. They aren't professional interviewers. They're controllers. They're accountants. They're finance people. We know what's going to fly and what's not going to fly. For example, it never helps to wear an ankle bracelet. It never helps for men to wear a bracelet. It never helps for men to use profanity in an interview. It never gets them the job. . . . Same with drinking a beer at lunch. Those are just things that we cover in an interview briefing to let them know what they need to do.

The strategy of minimizing negatives by not wearing a bracelet or avoiding alcohol is complemented by advice that candidates should present a positive tone and content during interviews. This includes reminding candidates that not everyone they meet during the interview will necessarily be in a selling mode and they may, in consequence, get asked the annoying "Why are you looking for a job?" question. Ted, for example, said he always anticipated this question when prepping candidates; he warned them to expect it and tried to get his candidates to dismiss it by reinterpreting it for them:

He [the candidate] goes on this interview, and they ask, "So what brings you to the employment marketplace, Jack? Why are you out looking for a job?" And he says, "What do you mean, why am I looking for a job? What did this recruiter say

to you? I'm minding my own business, I get a call from this
guy, he tells me about this great opportunity which he's been
selling all week. And you ask me why I'm looking for a job?"
And he gets aggravated. They get upset. They get mad. Here
they are being headhunted for a particular job, and the recruiter's telling them how wonderful the company is, bragging
on the company, to entice him to go on the interview, and
some twenty-eight-year-old personnel manager is saying, "So
why are you looking for a job?"

So I prepare them for all these questions, which will aggra-
vate them. And I say, "When you get that question, just translate it. Now I know you're not going to say you're not out
looking for a job. *I* know you're not out looking for a job. But
Suzie Q.'s been to some seminar conducted by some goofy psy-
chologist training her how to do these screen-out questions. So
she doesn't know better; she's not as bright as you or I. She
doesn't know better so she's asking questions that she was
taught in a seminar on how to screen people out. Don't let it
bother you when she says, 'Why are you out looking for a job?'
You simply translate that as meaning what would motivate
you to make a change from your company to their wonderful
company."

When answering this question, Ted said he always reminded candidates not to say anything negative about their current employer
and to keep the interview (and interviewer) focused on what was attractive about the new job:

In response to the why-are-you-looking question, I had one
candidate say, "I got a 3 percent raise and I thought I was due
for a 5 percent raise and it kind of annoyed me." I said, "You're
talking negatives. Don't say anything whatsoever which is negative or the interviewer will stop the process and probe that
negative, and probe and probe and break you down. Don't be a
sap. Don't jump to negatives. They don't want to hire somebody who's running away from a situation. They want to hire
somebody who's running toward their situation. So keep this
to yourself. I don't even want to hear the gruesome things
about your boss. I don't even want to hear the negative stuff. I
only want to hear positive words out of your mouth." So I

train them to say positive words. And then I have them repeat it back.

He gave an example of the kind of positive response he recommended his candidates provide:

> The reason you're interested in making a change or considering a change from the wonderful General Mills company to the wonderful Kellogg's company is because you got the call from the recruiter, commissioned by your company, in regard to this assignment. "I basically stood at attention because I recognize your company's a major force in the industry, a great company, a company whose business is going forward and not sideways. I understand that future career development is excellent, and that's what brings me here today. I'd like to hear more. Would you please tell me more? I'd like to hear more about the opportunities." Some answer like that.

Headhunters urge candidates to accentuate the positive for two main reasons. First, as Ted noted, headhunters believe clients want the new hire to be someone who is attracted by the new opportunity, not repelled by the old one. "Pull" factors are more desirable than "push" factors in the eyes of clients. Second, and more important, headhunters believe a positive approach enhances a candidate's "likability," and anything that makes a candidate more likable increases the chances of an offer. Likability, according to headhunters, is always a necessary selection criterion.

The observations headhunters offer on the critical importance of candidate likability are consistent with research on links between affective reactions, social cognition, and evaluations (e.g., Cardy and Dobbins 1986; Isen 1987; Keenan 1977). Robert Baron (1989) has argued that an interviewer who likes a candidate will be more likely to remember favorable information about the candidate, will interpret ambiguous information positively, and will be predisposed to rate the candidate as acceptable. Impression management thus shapes evaluations by inducing positive affect.

In addition to helping candidates strike the right tone during the interview, headhunters prep them on the content of what they will say during the interview. Headhunters encourage candidates to provide answers to questions in the form of specific accomplishments, either how they have saved money for their company or how they have made their company money. Ted said: "What they want is evidence that you're going to make or save their company money, because that's the bottom line." Well-crafted and well-delivered examples of accomplishments—especially those that provide meaningful metrics based on percentages or dollars—are that evidence. By getting candidates to be specific about their past performances, headhunters are also encouraging candidates to sell themselves. As we have noted, a recruited candidate is not necessarily an eager job seeker; headhunters worry that during the interview the candidate will present himself as a buyer rather than a seller. Ted explained that he tried to get candidates to imagine themselves as a "product":

> I say, "You are the product; you're selling the product. You want to provide the evidence from which the buyer draws a logical conclusion that they should hire you or they're nuts." I tell these people that every fifteen minutes during the interview I want you to ask yourself, Are you communicating key accomplishments [from] which they're drawing the logical conclusion that if they hire you, their company's going to make and save money?

If a candidate chafed at having to market himself in this manner and claimed that being headhunted gave him the freedom to be himself, Ted would remind him that he owed the company that was interviewing him a good performance:

> I say, "You are insulting them if you don't put on a show—and they're paying for a show. You know how much they're paying to fly you out from Owensboro, Kentucky, to Miami?
> "How much?"
> "The round-trip fare is one thousand dollars. You know how much it costs to go see a Broadway play? Sixty-five dollars. So he's expecting at least ten times the value of a Broadway play. He's paying one thousand dollars for you to come and put a show on. If you don't put a show on, he's going to be insulted. He wants to hear what you have to offer; he wants to hear it."

The notion that candidates need to sell themselves governs how headhunters view the salary question. Headhunters tell candidates not to bring up salary or benefits issues on a first interview because it conveys the impression that they are more interested in what they could *get* from the company than what they would *give* to the organization.

Specific Prepping: What the Books Don't Contain

General prepping is aimed at helping candidates perform well in a variety of interviews. Specific prepping, in contrast, is geared toward boosting performance in an interview for a particular job and with a particular hiring manager. It typically includes a mix of information about the interviewers and their backgrounds, their way of conducting interviews, questions that might be asked, the sequence of events likely to occur during the interview, and hot-button issues. This information is invaluable because it is not readily available from any other source. Popular job-finding books such as *What Color Is Your Parachute?* do not contain anything like the specific advice provided by headhunters. Personal contacts—friends, relatives, and acquaintances—might be able to supply some of this inside information, but they are highly unlikely to know nearly as much as headhunters about the interview cycle, the key decision makers, and the hot buttons. The sheer frequency with which headhunters are in contact with clients allows them to amass a quantity and quality of information about employers that cannot be matched by a casual or occasional observer of the hiring process.

One objective of specific prepping is to make the candidate as familiar as possible with the interviewers and interview procedure, as Dale explained:

> We say, "Hey, this is what's going to take place tomorrow. This is who you're going to talk to. This is a little bit of information about the company and the position. Here's a little bit of insight on the people you're going to be interviewing with, okay." So we just try to familiarize him with the process, and what to expect, and make him feel at ease. . . . "This is a little bit about Bill [the interviewer]. He seems to be somewhat quiet, but don't take that personally. Or he may be very aggressive, and he may be very short, but he's a busy person. He's a

nice guy. He's just a very busy person, so he doesn't spend as much time with people. So once again, don't take that personally." So it's just little things like that, so they can keep their mind at ease.

Doug alerts candidates to possible faux pas: "I try to find out as much about the personalities as I can. Try to find out where they went to school and what area of the country they're from so that I can tell the candidate that, make sure they don't step on their toes by saying, 'Well, those doggone Clemson grads,' or whatever it is."

Context-specific information of this sort is obtained from clients through pre- and post-interview questioning; it can also be obtained from candidates through the same kind of reconnaissance used by headhunters to discover and construct hot buttons. George explained how a debriefing session with a first candidate can be used to prepare subsequent candidates for a particularly difficult interviewer:

> Sometimes the candidate comes out and says, That guy's a jerk; he sat there the whole time and belittled me and my résumé. . . . What you try to do is turn it into a positive. You go back to the candidates that are going in next and say, Look, the guy interviews, and we have a lot of clients do this that will interview on a negative approach. . . . So the guy's prepared for it when he gets in there, and he's mentally already thought of ways to get the guy off of that type thing.

The widespread use of candidate reconnaissance by headhunters casts doubt on an argument advanced by Robert Dipboye and Barbara Gaugler. They suggested that "structured interviews may discourage impression management" because "the opportunities for applicants to manipulate and shape the interviewer's impressions in a favorable direction are limited by the standardization of questioning" (1993, 149). We find, in contrast, that candidate reconnaissance is even more effective in helping headhunters shape the impression-management strategies of subsequent candidates when interviews have a structured, predictable format.

Headhunters cover three main topics during their specific prepping of candidates: questions that will be asked during the interview, chemistry, and hot buttons. Here is how Walter, for example, prepped

Gary, his top candidate for the taxation director's position at Office Depot, for the questions likely to come up during the interview. Walter began with a brief description of Jay, the main interviewer: a CPA, in his middle thirties, from the West Coast, had four children, and was "a very open, good guy, looks like Mr. Surfer." Walter told Gary he would probably be asked four questions during the interview. The first would be to tell the interviewer a little more about himself, that is, to flesh out his résumé. He recommended that Gary prepare a two- to three-minute response to this question by writing out on a piece of paper his résumé in reverse, beginning with his education and moving chronologically forward from there. He told Gary to remember to be broad; "perhaps ask Jay if there is anything he would like you to emphasize." He reminded Gary that his goal was to develop a relationship with Jay: "What you want to do is establish a dialogue as quickly as possible." Gary should therefore avoid talking about himself at length. Walter told him to highlight his law degree, his master's degree in taxation, and his international experience: "They want someone with the horsepower to do some serious strategic planning." He continued: "They don't want a manager—it's easy for them to find someone to manage the tax department—they want a thinker. I hate to use the word 'intellectual' because that's a loaded term in business, but that's sort of what they're looking for."

The second question, Walter said, was a potential minefield because it would be about Gary's motivation and might lead to the topic of remuneration. Gary should avoid the topic of money at all costs because it could easily destroy a developing relationship. Walter explained to Gary that "money in our culture has a power that used to be attributed to religion." He thought it unlikely that Jay would raise the salary question; if he did, Gary should "segue right past it" by stating that he wants to be treated fairly but money is not his primary motivation. What Gary should say is that he is looking for a place where he can grow professionally, make a contribution and be recognized, and raise his family. In other words, a home rather than a place to make a quick buck.

Walter prefaced his remarks about the third question by saying he "hates" this particular one. He said that Jay would say, "Gee, Gary, we've talked a lot about your strengths. What are your weaknesses?" Walter joked, "What are you going to say—that you drink on weekends, you're a psychopath?" He told Gary not to say he was a workaholic—that's a cliché. His advice was that Gary should say he had to learn the hard way how to delegate responsibility: how not to hover over people but also how not to give too much leeway. He should tell Jay that it had taken him several years to learn how to manage effectively but that he was now pretty good at it. Another suggestion Walter offered was that Gary should say that the first time he did an employee-performance review, he did a lousy job; this is a good "weakness" because almost everyone does these reviews poorly at first.

Finally, Jay would ask Gary if he had any further questions. Walter told Gary to answer this question with question: "Based on my résumé, how do I fit what you're looking for?" Walter instructed Gary to ask that question and then pause; the pause, he said, would help force a response from Jay. He explained that what Gary would hope to hear is some remark to the effect that "I hoped you had more X in your background." Gary could then respond by saying, "I'm glad you brought that up. I didn't have time to cover everything when I told you about myself. Let me tell you about my experience with X." This is a tactic for neutralizing reservations. Alternatively, Walter said, if Jay expressed interest in you, that would give you the chance to say how much you want to work for Office Depot. Remember, Walter emphasized, they want to be liked, just as you want to be liked: "It's just like when you were fourteen and you wanted to know if the girl wanted to kiss you. People don't change that much."

The second topic covered in specific prepping is chemistry. The emergence of good chemistry between a candidate and key members of the hiring company is often the product of chance similarities. Chance in this case involves both the possession and perception of chemistry-relevant attributes. Headhunters attempt to control chance, first, by identifying candidates who possess these attributes and, second, by working to ensure that those attributes are perceived by the client. The first step is straightforward, as Ted explained: "I try to get somebody who has similar features, similar background, similar personality as the person who's interviewing them. That's the ideal goal if you can do it."

Headhunters are emphatic, however, in claiming that it is not sufficient for a candidate to possess chemistry-enhancing attributes since many background experiences, personality characteristics, values, and interests that could influence the emergence of good chemistry might not be recognized or be known by candidates and interviewers. They might not surface spontaneously during an interview in a way that would allow them to influence the perceived chemistry. Interviews, after all, provide only a glimpse into a candidate's thought, conduct, and background. Candidates with inside information on the interviewers and the organization's culture can deliberately accentuate those factors that are known to produce good chemistry, thereby reducing the element of luck. Scott stated: "I let them know what the company culture is. Try to give them the personalities of the people they'll be interviewing with so they go in saying, 'I know what turns this guy on.'"

Headhunters, accordingly, prep candidates for chemistry by identifying and pointing out various experiences or traits that will establish a common point of reference between the candidate and the hiring manager (and any other interviewers). Headhunters implicitly strive to produce the widely recognized "similar-to-me" effect (Rand and Wexley 1975) by alerting candidates to the social similarities they should signal during the interview. Given the tendency for people to like those they believe are similar to themselves, and the previously mentioned effect of liking on evaluations, the establishment of social similarities can be quite consequential, as other researchers have noted (Lin, Dobbins, and Farh 1992). In this connection, consider how Scott summarized his approach to prepping and its intended effects:

> I don't know if you've ever heard of the three-minute interview where the guy comes in and the interviewee says, "Tell me about the position first." And then he takes his skills and matches it to what the hiring authority says. That's my job as a headhunter. I give candidates the three-minute interview. They walk in knowing this guy did this, this guy went to the University of Tennessee, you went to Kentucky, or whatever. They hit it off. All the little intangible things that usually get people hired by luck, I give them.

Overlapping college affiliations and previous employers were often cited as well-known chemistry enhancers, which headhunters like George seek to discover and disclose to both candidates and clients:

> When I start to work with you [a client], the first thing I'm going to ask you is what your background is. And if you say, "Well, I worked with IBM or with Dow Chemical or I came

from Procter and Gamble," or whatever the case may be, "and I
have an MBA from Indiana or Georgia," or wherever, I keep my
eye out for people that maybe have worked at companies like
that. I've got one client who is a Villanova grad. Well, I know
that if I get a Villanova grad, he'd want to talk to them. So
when I get Villanova people, I call him and say, "Look, I've got
a Villanova person."

Knowledge of or participation in various leisure activities and sports
is also frequently noted as a chemistry enhancer. This information
can easily be worked into the headhunter's next conversation with
his client, as Walter did when he learned that a candidate enjoyed
golf. Knowing that the hiring manager was an avid golfer as well, he
made casual mention of their common interest in golf during the
conversation in which he set up the interview, thereby planting a
chemistry-enhancing seed. Walter was ensuring that their shared
hobby was not overlooked, even if neither client nor candidate
brought it up during the interview. Similarly, he said he was going to
make certain that Jay, the Office Depot interviewer, knew before the
interview with Gary that Gary, like Jay, was Jewish. (Gary was in fact
subsequently hired by Office Depot.) As far as headhunters are concerned, therefore, the apparent luck reflected in a common interest
that becomes a conversational icebreaker, or even better, the basis for
rapport, can be controlled to some extent by gathering and sharing detailed information.

Good chemistry also stems from what headhunters refer to as a
candidate's "personality." Headhunters recognize that some aspects
of a candidate's presentation of self are simply not malleable: they are
unlikely to change, regardless of how much advice or coaching the
candidate receives. For example, Ted discussed the problems he was
experiencing with a candidate who lacked a "forceful" personality:
"I'm dealing with a guy right now who's going on an interview, and
I've already had him on five interviews. He's blown each one. They
really should hire him. But he's not a forceful personality; that's the
only negative. So I've given him tips to try to be more forceful, because I know he's a good person, but because he's not forceful, the
companies are hesitating about hiring him." Those who lack forceful
personalities cannot easily alter their presentations of self and will
not fit clients that have this attribute as a selection criterion. Diffi-

dent candidates do have their uses for headhunters, however, assuming the latter have been successful in generating other candidates with the right kind of personality. They allow headhunters to offer clients a choice of candidates, which is what most clients prefer (see chapter 5). They can perform the client reconnaissance that allows headhunters to form a sharper picture of hot buttons and chemistry (see chapter 6) that in turn enable them to do a better job of prepping later candidates. Finally, they can be stockpiled in the hope that a client that does not have forcefulness as a hiring requirement will eventually materialize.

Nevertheless, headhunters believe many aspects of self-presentation that are commonly attributed to personality can be modified through prepping. For example, several headhunters spoke of the importance of candidates "asking for the job," of expressing serious, almost aggressive, interest in a position. If a headhunter knows that a hiring manager wants candidates to be eager, candidates can be prepped to meet that need, as Karen noted:

> I will give them [the candidate] the benefit of my knowledge of
> that person [the hiring manager] and what they're looking for.
> Why they are looking, why the last person didn't fit, and what
> they didn't like about other candidates. You can be sure I'm
> going to prep them. If a hiring manager says that the others
> have been too laid-back, I'm going to go to my candidate and
> say, "Listen—don't you be timid. Go in there and ask for the
> job."

Thus, knowledge of a hiring manager allows a headhunter to suggest that a candidate conduct himself in a particular way for a particular interview. Behavior and expressions that a client might think are inherent in a candidate's personality may well be a mask a candidate is wearing at a headhunter's bidding.

In the third part of specific prepping, headhunters instruct candidates about the client's hot buttons, as Henry described:

> I cover who the company is and what they're looking for and
> what some of the idiosyncrasies of the company are. I tell them
> that the critical parts of the search are this, this, and that, and
> make darn sure in the course of the interview that you have an

opportunity to point out to them that you have that experience. This company is very concerned about shrink control. So
it's important that you be prepared to explain to them what
kind of successes that you've had in the area of shrink control
because that's a critical factor why they're looking for somebody here. And so I'll prep them.

Headhunters insist that hot-button prepping is not intended to give a
candidate the apparent ability to press hot buttons that she is actually incapable of pressing. Instead, they want to ensure that a candidate lets the client know she has the right skills and experience; they
fear that, left to her own devices, a candidate might not effectively
display that she has what the client wants. Like chemistry-related attributes, hot-button talents cannot help a candidate obtain an offer if
the client fails to perceive them. Prepping a candidate on the hot-button issues helps her be prepared to summarize skills and experiences
and to show how they meet the employer's needs. In Dale's words, "I
try to help bring out the best in them." Michelle made a similar point
in the course of a long discussion about how and why she engaged in
candidate prep: "I mean, we're grooming people so they put their best
foot forward. Not so much so that we're trying to change who they
are and they're going to turn into this monster two days later. *It's just
that everything in life is presentation* [Michelle's emphasis]. And if
something is presented more favorably, people feel better about buying it. And it's just marketing and packaging."

Indirect impression management—general and specific prepping—
represents the best efforts of headhunters to manipulate and control
what is for them the most uncertain and most unpredictable moment
in their business: the meeting of client and candidate. All their attempts to control the recruitment process before and after the interview will result in a placement only if the interview goes well, so it is
small wonder that they go to such lengths to manage the impressions
that each party forms of the other during the interview. Bringing
client and candidate together and managing the impressions they
form of each other do not, however, mark the end of the headhunter's
work. If the meeting goes well and the client wants to offer the candidate the job, headhunters have to make sure the offer is accepted.
Managing the job offer and getting it accepted take headhunters into
the delicate and tricky endgame of matchmaking.

8

From Bridges to Buffers

Closing the Double Sale

> The thing that's very unique about our business is if I'm selling
> chairs, once I convince you to buy the chair, it's a done deal.
> The chair's not going to change its mind. [What's] unique about
> our business is that once I convince you, I've got this other per-
> son over here thinking, I've got some concerns, and I've got to
> work them together until they're a perfect match.
>
> —George, A Southern City headhunter

Headhunters bridge the gap, or fill the structural hole, between client
and candidate in various ways. In arranging a job interview, a headhunter brings together two parties who might otherwise have re-
mained unacquainted; in prepping them for the interview, she attempts to increase the chances of each finding the other attractive
and desirable. The job interview, however, changes the relationship
between client and candidate, who no longer face each other as un-
knowns. By the same token, the headhunter's role is now also quali-
tatively different; she becomes an intermediary between two parties
who are quite familiar with each other, a role that mimics that of investment bankers who mediate between companies and investors
(Eccles and Crane 1988), venture capitalists who mediate between entrepreneurs and managers (Stross 2000), and securities analysts who
mediate between companies and share buyers (Zuckerman 1999).

In every one of these settings the intermediary links parties that,
though aware of the existence of the other, require the transaction to
be legitimated before they consummate it. The intermediaries are the
legitimators. Take, for example, Ezra Zuckerman's analysis of "coverage mismatch," the extent to which a company that does business in
a particular industry is *not* covered by the securities analysts who

specialize in that industry. Zuckerman reports that the greater the coverage mismatch, the lower the company's stock price, indicating that investors are reluctant to purchase the shares of an undercovered company. Similarly, entrepreneurs need venture capitalists not just to provide capital (which, in fact, may not even be needed) but to certify to prospective managers who are contemplating joining the new organization that it has been evaluated and passed muster (Stross 2000).

Although headhunters also legitimate transactions, the double sale complicates their role. The client may have been persuaded to buy the product (the candidate), but there is no sale until the product has accepted the client. Getting a candidate to accept a job offer is the final and, for any headhunter, most perilous stage of making a placement. Headhunters know it is easier to talk candidates into considering a new opportunity than it is to persuade them to grasp that opportunity. From the interview to the offer to the acceptance much can and does go awry. A candidate may feel he was insufficiently wooed during the interview and consequently spurns the offer when it is made. A candidate may be simply using the interview as an opportunity to gauge her labor-market value or simply to do some "window-shopping." A candidate may be willing to accept the offer, but his family may refuse to relocate. A candidate may decide to accept a counteroffer from her current employer. Finally, a candidate may simply be fearful of leaving a familiar work setting and starting afresh elsewhere.

Headhunters cope with the problem of getting candidates to accept job offers in two ways. First, they make an effort to keep client and candidate apart after the job interview: they insert themselves as a buffer between the two parties. Headhunters attempt to play the part of intermediary so completely that all contact between client and candidate flows through them. One implication of their new role as buffer is that the structural-hole argument is turned on its head: headhunters now *create* the structural hole between the parties. Headhunters want to keep the two sides apart in order to control their interactions. They believe that if client and candidate were to negotiate directly, the sale would be jeopardized because contact might lead to friction; by keeping them apart, headhunters hope to close each separately and simultaneously on terms acceptable to each. Second, headhunters attempt to assert psychological control over candidates by playing on the fears and insecurities that job offers commonly induce in candidates. For example, a headhunter may claim that a candidate will jeopardize his career if he turns down an offer in favor of a counteroffer from his original employer. Headhunters behave like the litigators portrayed by Jennifer Pierce (1995): they use strategic friendliness and intimidation to manipulate the emotions of others.

Closing the deal is a four-step process for headhunters. First, they have to sustain candidate interest in the job so that when an offer is made, it is likely to be welcomed. Second, they must manage the presentation of the offer so that both client and candidate feel like winners. Third, they must counter the counteroffer in order to avoid losing candidates to their current employers. And fourth, they must manage the resignation in order to overcome any last-minute doubts and fears a candidate may have about cutting ties with the old employer.

Sustaining Candidate Interest

After the adrenaline high of the interview, candidate interest in a position inevitably wanes, at least slightly. Unless the candidate is offered the job during or at the conclusion of the interview, which is improbable, he must wait for the offer. As the passage of time cools the enthusiasm of the candidate, it becomes more likely he will turn down the offer. Headhunters cope with this difficulty through the tactic of repeated or continual "closing." Closing entails reminding candidates (or, more accurately, getting candidates to remind themselves) why they were interested in the job in the first place, keeping candidates in a state of anticipation so they will respond eagerly to the job offer if and when it is made, and finding out whether there are any unforeseen difficulties that might lead to the offer's being declined.

Experienced headhunters know that reminding candidates of their interest in the job is a process that begins when they contact prospects and probe for the wounds that will convert them into candidates. In the post-interview phase headhunters work to keep these concerns alive by reminding candidates of their wounds and then encouraging them to come to the realization that the only way they can obtain relief is by making a job change.

Headhunters attempt to guide candidates to the job-change decision so that they feel they made it on their own. At this point in the process headhunters rely on friendliness to achieve their objectives, presenting themselves as the candidate's counselor and creating the illusion of disinterest but all the while steering the candidate in a particular direction. Gene explained that using a hard or "push" sell here was ineffective because a candidate would not feel responsible for the decision and, therefore, would be more likely to retract it. Instead, he and other headhunters practice the art of "pull" selling, closing off a candidate's options so the candidate makes the decision the headhunter wants without being aware of the latter's guiding hand. The process consists of a series of closes, all taking the candidate closer to the point where she will accept the job offer if it is made. Gene described the closing sequence:

> It's [with] the very first close [i.e., when the headhunter informs a potential candidate of an actual or possible job opportunity] that you determine whether there's any interest. And if there is: "Do you want me to call you back?"
> "Yes."
> Okay, that's a closure. You come back with this other information and you say, "When we last spoke, you said that if this, this, and this, you wanted to hear more. Is that still the case?"
> "Yes."
> Okay, another piece of closure. You go to the next level, and you keep going, say, "Okay, if you go to this opportunity and they're everything I've described to you, then are you . . . ?" It's what I call pre-positioning, so you get all these affirmations.

Headhunters reason if that these closes have worked, they will have cut off a candidate's "escape routes," leaving only one option: to accept the offer.

Even when a candidate is enthusiastic about getting the offer, headhunters are well aware that it may still be declined. Family considerations frequently intrude: a candidate may want to take the job but may be unable to persuade the spouse and/or children to move. A headhunter may make a point of "accidentally" contacting the candidate's spouse, calling the candidate's home at a time when she knows the candidate will not be there, to verify the spouse's willingness to relocate.

Headhunters would rather not have an offer made than have the candidate turn it down. As we pointed out in chapter 3, clients expect their offers to be accepted and blame headhunters if they are declined. Headhunters can use this factor to their advantage by discouraging clients from making offers to candidates they think are unlikely to accept them. This course of action allows headhunters to portray themselves as loyal agents of their clients.

Managing the Offer

The skill in managing an offer is to ensure, first, that neither client nor candidate gets offended by the other's response during the period immediately after the offer is made and, second, that client and candidate each feels like a winner. When an offer is initially made, both client and candidate have high expectations. Although headhunters want this result, they recognize that the higher the expectations, the greater the dismay if either party does not respond in a manner commensurate with the other's expectations. The biggest potential source of disappointment is money. In many cases a candidate does not know before the offer exactly what the salary for the position is. This situation typically occurs when an employer states a job's salary in terms of a range, for example, the position pays $50,000 to $60,000 a year; the not-surprising result is that a candidate expects to receive a salary of close to $60,000 and is acutely disappointed if the offer is nearer $50,000. Employers list salaries in ranges because it gives them flexibility should they decide that the candidate they really want is particularly well qualified (or well paid) and, therefore, needs an extra inducement to take the job. Normally, however, they do not anticipate having to pay top dollar in their range to make the hire.

Headhunters are all too aware that when an offer falls short of a candidate's expectations, the chances of a placement are considerably diminished. In cases of this kind, hurt feelings and recriminations quickly supplant the goodwill that had been established between employer and candidate; as the deal collapses, the headhunter not only loses a fee but is likely to be blamed by both sides. The problem, as headhunters were quick to acknowledge, is that a person's salary has both a practical and a symbolic importance. As Ted said, "This salary business is a measure of one's worth." A difference of as little as $1,000 or $2,000 a year between what a candidate expects and what he is offered may have little practical effect on a candidate's lifestyle, but the candidate is likely to interpret it as a signal that he is not as valued a catch as he had imagined. Headhunters often compare recruitment and hiring to engagement and marriage; the moment when a candidate accepts an offer is equivalent to when the spouses say "I do." Continuing the metaphor, an offer that is declined because the candidate was not offered enough money is equivalent to one partner breaking off the engagement after telling the other, "You don't love me enough."

Headhunters have adopted two strategies for dealing with the money problem. The first is to keep client and candidate from discussing salary issues for as long as possible. Headhunters advise their candidates not to bring up this topic during the interview; should a client ask a candidate how much she wants or expects to earn, she should sidestep the question by responding that money is not the reason she is interested in the job. Second, a headhunter engages in pre-offer negotiations with both client and candidate to come up with a figure he knows is acceptable to both parties. Take, for example, a position in which the salary is listed as being between $50,000 and $60,000. Assume the top candidate is someone earning $52,000 who is seeking a 10 percent salary increase, or a salary of around $57,000. The employer, however, feels that the salary offer should be no more than $54,000. Under these circumstances the headhunter tries to get client and candidate to commit to a compromise salary of, say, $56,000. He asks the client if he wishes not to make the offer for the sake of saving $2,000 and the candidate if she wishes to decline the offer because it is $1,000 less than what she hoped to get. The purpose of the headhunter's involvement here is to prevent client and candidate from confronting each other over salary differences that are symbolic rather than substantial. By asking both of them whether they want to abandon the deal because of a disagreement over a couple of thousand dollars, the headhunter is trying to push the symbolic element of salary into the background and to get the parties to focus on bridging the relatively small dollar gap that separates them.

One trick some headhunters use to forestall a candidate's sense of disappointment over receiving a salary that might be less than she had hoped for is what is known as the "two-tier close." The headhunter closes the candidate at a figure he knows is lower than the offer. In the example just given he might close the candidate at $55,000 after he has already persuaded the client to commit to $56,000. When the offer is made, the candidate learns she is going to get more than she expected, thus making her feel indebted to her headhunter for getting her more money and for making her a winner in her negotiations with her new employer. It makes the headhunter appear to be her ally.

One headhunter explained how to use the drama of an incipient job offer in combination with the two-tier close to put a positive spin on the offer. In this excerpt from our fieldnotes he describes how he manipulates the candidate's emotions with the hoary good-news-bad-news line, which, he points out, also makes him look good in the candidate's eyes:

> I am sitting in Martin's office when he tells me, with mock trepidation—"I don't know if I should tell you this if it's going to appear in print"—that he is going to explain how the two-tier close works. This is how it works, he says. The company agrees to make an offer to a candidate at $38K. The recruiter calls the candidate and says that he has a message in his hand to call HR at the company; the HR manager is going to a meeting at 2:30 P.M., and it is now 2:25 P.M. The recruiter tells the candidate that an offer might be forthcoming, and he gets the candidate's authority to accept the offer at $36K (i.e., $2,000 lower than he knows the offer will be). The recruiter waits five minutes—while the candidate is in a state of suspense—and then calls the candidate back with an "I've got good news and I've got bad news" statement. "The bad news is that I couldn't get you $36K. The good news is that I got you $38K." The beauty of the two-tier close is that it makes the recruiter look good and makes the candidate even more enthusiastic about the job offer.

A headhunter tries to make sure client and candidate negotiate with her rather than with each other. If they were to face each other directly, the inherent emotionality of a salary disagreement—the you-don't-love-me-enough component to these disputes—would be more likely to surface, making a compromise much more difficult to realize. By inserting himself as the go-between, the headhunter offers himself as the outlet for their frustration and anger: he absorbs the heat when negotiations get heated. As Gene liked to say, "The recruiter wears the asbestos suit." As the outside but interested third party, the headhunter is not offended by low-ball salary offers or avaricious candidates and is not inclined to walk away from the deal in a fit of pique. Instead, his incentive is to ride out the emotional turbulence and then to get each side to commit to a mutually acceptable salary. His hope is that when the offer is made, it will be exactly what the candidate expected and in fact has agreed to and will, therefore, be accepted.

If they have any choice in the matter, headhunters prefer to be the ones to deliver offers to candidates and acceptances to clients. Ideally, they would keep client and candidate apart from the interview until the day the latter reports for work. Some clients allow headhunters to make the offers, but many insist on doing it themselves. If clients are the ones making the offers, headhunters encourage them to be positive and upbeat. We listened to Gene telling a client that the offer letter should have a "congratulatory tone" and should not be full of contingencies such as verification of references, education, and employment history. He argued that the candidate would understand without having to be told that the offer was contingent on these factors; it set the wrong tone to bring them up in the offer letter.

Friendliness, or a headhunter's pretending to be on the candidate's side, is an effective tactic for getting a candidate receptive to and interested in an offer. If, however, the candidate is a valued employee, his employer will in all likelihood match the offer with a counteroffer. Counteroffers are inherently appealing to candidates because they satisfy some of their needs, such as a salary increase or a promotion, without the strain of changing employers. To counter the counteroffers, headhunters turn to a stronger weapon than friendliness: they use intimidation, attempting to frighten candidates into declining counteroffers.

Countering the Counteroffer

Every headhunter fears counteroffers. One of the many ironies of headhunting is that the better the candidate and the more likely, therefore, the offer, the stronger the counteroffer and the more determined the efforts to retain that employee. By being successful in recruitment, headhunters increase the odds of their failure in placement. The economic boom of the 1990s, allied to the downsizing of many U.S. companies during the same period, made headhunters' tasks even more difficult as these organizations redoubled their ef-

forts to keep what was in many cases a smaller group of more important employees.

The carrot in the counteroffer is invariably money. George, who
told us he had lost at least two big deals in the first half of 1995 to
counteroffers, said the combination of a strong market, low unem-
ployment, and corporate competitiveness had resulted in "tremen-
dous counteroffers going around." Headhunters, therefore, devote
much of their countering-the-countcroffer strategy to minimizing the
importance of money in the job-change decision.

When headhunters persuade candidates to change jobs, they expect that candidates will earn more in their new jobs than they did in
their old jobs. Notwithstanding headhunters' disavowal of the
salience of money as a wound, they know that money matters, as we
established in the preceding section. Failure to obtain a salary increase for a candidate usually results in the offer's rejection—lateral
offers (and job changes) are quite rare—but if the main attraction of
an offer is its salary, it is vulnerable to the response of a counteroffer.
Headhunters also know that the easiest part of an offer to counter is
its salary: candidates, left to their own counsel, will seldom embrace
the uncertainty of a job change if they can earn the same amount (or
even slightly more) by staying put. Headhunters cope with this problem by telling candidates to expect a counteroffer and by denying its
legitimacy.

Headhunters alert candidates to the possibility of a counteroffer
because they want to prepare candidates for it and because they want
to trivialize it. They want candidates to interpret it as a mundane ges-
ture that employers routinely make and not as an extraordinary response to the threatened departure of a valued employee. They want
candidates to think of it as merely a bribe. Here, for example, is
George's explanation of how he copes with counteroffers:

> Well, you try to basically forewarn them [the candidate] and
> tell them what's going to happen, tell them what they're going
> to say. I have a deal right now the client says I know they're
> going to counteroffer. I said, Well, yeah, that's true, but we're
> going to get him prepared. . . . And they [the current employers]
> all say the same thing in so many words and basically tell them
> what they're going to offer, more money, whatever. And I try to
> get them [the candidates] to realize what they're trying to do is
> buy them back.

Headhunters know counteroffers appeal to employees' insecurity and vanity. Everyone wants to be loved, is a favorite headhunter saying, and a counteroffer, unless deflated, readily appears to a candidate to be genuine commitment and affection. Headhunters want their candidates to see it instead as a tawdry and cynical response by an employer who has neglected the employee and who now wants to avoid the inconvenience and difficulty of finding a replacement. Henry claimed that preparation alone was sufficient to discredit counteroffers:

> Everybody wants to be wanted. And when your boss comes up
> to you and gives you that hug and says, "Gosh, you're the most
> fabulous person, how could we have overlooked you? My good-
> ness, how have we done this to you?" If you're forewarned that
> that's going to happen, then they're somewhat caustic going in
> and you don't normally have a problem with it. When you
> don't do it that way, then you get counteroffer problems.

Headhunters stress that telling candidates that all employers make counteroffers is effective only if it *precedes* the counteroffer. In this case the candidate is psychologically prepared to receive, and ultimately reject, the counteroffer. Headhunters want candidates to be thinking, when the counteroffer is made, "Aha, Henry [the head-hunter] told me about this. He said to be aware of this." Once the counteroffer is made, however, it is too late to warn candidates: "If you tell them after the fact, then it's sour grapes."

For most headhunters, thwarting counteroffers rests on a combination of anticipation and information, that is, how they decode counteroffers for candidates. There are two points of information they are particularly eager to impress on candidates. Both are designed to get the candidate to question the legitimacy and good faith of the counteroffer and to worry that his career will be harmed if he accepts it. First, headhunters say, a counteroffer is really a malicious confidence trick dressed up as a bribe. Employers have no intention of retaining, over the long term, employees to whom they have made counteroffers. They simply want to delay the departure of an employee—to buy some time before the employee eventually leaves (either voluntarily or involuntarily). Departure is virtually inevitable, they argue. Every headhunter with whom we discussed counteroffers reported that he made the following claim to candidates who received counteroffers:

"Statistics show" that 80 percent (sometimes it was 85 percent) of employees who accept a counteroffer are not with the same company one year later. It is better, headhunters therefore advise, to take the new offer and leave now than to wait six or nine months and leave under what may be far less favorable circumstances.

The second point headhunters make is that employers will find a way of punishing employees who have accepted counteroffers because these employees have betrayed them by receiving offers and have blackmailed them into making counteroffers. The punishment for "disloyalty," headhunters warn candidates, may include not getting future salary increases and promotions and even being fired for, as Ted colorfully put it, "fucking your boss." Ted said he cautioned any candidate contemplating a counteroffer to expect to lose his job if he accepted it: "And know what's going to happen when you say, yes, I'll stay. They're going to immediately plan for you to leave; they're going to plan for you to leave. . . . As soon as they find your replacement, they'll drum up some charges against you and let you go." If the candidate protested that this would not happen to him, Ted would respond with his favorite you-fucked-your-boss anecdote. The story was based, he claimed, on his own pre-headhunting experiences working as a manager of recruiting personnel for a major food manufacturer. It involved a company engineer who had received an offer, which had been matched by a counteroffer, including a 7 percent raise, that the engineer had accepted. Ted then contacted a couple of recruiters and asked them to find a replacement for this employee:

> So I said [explaining what he was saying to the candidate for
> whose benefit the story was being told], what's going to happen
> is we're going to Friday, after we get the acceptance [from the
> replacement], the starting date, we'll call the man in and tell
> him he's being released. And he'll be wanting to know why,
> and it's because of disloyalty. You know how the company feels
> about disloyalty: you were on an interview obviously nine
> months earlier—you took it on company time.

Ted subsequently encountered the terminated employee in the parking lot and explained to him what happened:

> I said, "I don't know about you, but I grew up in Providence,
> Rhode Island, and I don't know, maybe it's the neighborhood I

grew up in. I just know one thing: if you fuck someone, they'll fuck you back—and you fucked your boss.

[Employee:] "What do you mean I fucked my boss?"

I said, "You put a gun to his head. You said that if you don't give me a raise, I'm leaving. Don't you think he remembers that? Pissed him off. You would have been better off to have simply gone in, laid your resignation down, and kept your word. He'd have had more respect for you; he might end up being a good friend of yours as years go by. But as the months have gone on, this business about your putting a shotgun to his head."

[Employee:] "I put a shotgun to his head?"

"Yes, you put a shotgun to his head and told him you'd stay if he gave you a raise, in effect is what you said. So you just robbed him, highway robbery. He'll remember that. . . . Don't you think that when he gets a chance to get his revenge, he's going to do it? . . . And you can't say you weren't on an interview, you can't say you weren't using company time to go on that interview. You were disloyal; we can't have disloyal people working here. Sorry."

Ted acknowledged that his story was possibly somewhat apocryphal. "How much of it is factual after all these years?" was his rhetorical question after recounting it. But, he continued, it didn't really matter how accurate it was. Its purpose was to scare candidates away from accepting a counteroffer by suggesting what might happen to them if they did: "The point that matters [is] that [it] gets their attention." Karen said, "You try to put that fear in them, that you're a valued candidate now but if you accept a counteroffer, forget it, you will never be considered loyal, ever."

Having painted a scary picture for the candidate of his probable fate if he accepts a counteroffer, the headhunter then reminds the candidate that the reason he is considering the job offer is because of the wounds inflicted by his original employer. Even if he accepts the counteroffer, those wounds are not likely to heal, as Doug noted: "Just giving somebody more money does not address those concerns. If the problems are with your boss, your boss's boss, or anything like that, that hasn't changed." A new job at a new organization is the only certain way to surmount these problems. Gene uses a diagram to explain to his candidates the difference between a new offer and a counteroffer. He gives candidates a paper and pen and asks them to draw a straight line across the page. He then has them draw a ladder leading up to left side of the line; on the right side they draw a ladder above the line. The left ladder represents a candidate's present company: she is at the top of this ladder. The right ladder represents the new company: she is at the bottom of this ladder. The purpose of this simple illustration is get the candidate to appreciate that although a counteroffer may match a new offer, it is not in fact equivalent because the counteroffer is the culmination of one career whereas the new offer is the beginning of another.

Managing the Resignation

No headhunter is entirely secure about her placement (and fee) until the candidate shows up for work on the first day of the new job. All the psychological bracing in which headhunters have been engaged in countering the counteroffer is in vain if the candidate cannot actually bring himself or herself to walk through the door on that first day.[1] Although many if not most candidates are eager to begin the new job once they have decided to leave their current employer, not everyone finds it quite so easy to sever this "umbilical cord." It is long-term employees in particular who headhunters believe are most likely to suffer from cold feet. (We heard one industry trainer tell a group of consultants that he had a policy of not recruiting employees with more than seven years' tenure at their current employers because he believed anyone in this category had probably declined job offers in the past and, therefore, was unlikely to accept one in the future. Although none of the headhunters we interviewed or observed indicated that he or she followed quite so rigid a policy, long-term employees were viewed as difficult recruits.) Further, headhunters argue, even the most eager job changers experience at least some momentary trepidation as they contemplate the prospect of starting over at a different organization.

Headhunters have developed a two-pronged strategy to minimize

---

[1] Or if he walks back out after walking in. One of Karen's horror stories involved a candidate who accepted a position with one of her clients and then took some vacation time from his old employer to attend a sales meeting with his new colleagues. After being introduced as the new sales manager for Boston and sitting through the meeting, he returned to his original company and decided not to resign.

the risk of a last-minute letdown. First, they attempt to normalize the anxiety that candidates feel about changing jobs by suggesting that this reaction is commonplace. The fear of change, they say, afflicts everyone, no matter whether the candidate is a $20,000-a-year secretary or a $200,000-a-year corporate vice president. By suggesting that this anxiety is normal, headhunters seek to downplay its significance for candidates so they interpret it not as a special message or signal but as a conventional human response to a new environment. Fear that is normal and conventional, headhunters are implying, is not a sufficient reason for not taking the new job.

Second, headhunters attempt to ensure that the resignation meeting—where the candidate announces her intention to quit—is both short and unemotional. They believe a prolonged, sentimental meeting will only intensify a candidate's fear of change and could even make him or her feel guilty about leaving. In some cases a headhunter literally scripts a candidate's departure, telling her what to say or write and, more important, what not to say or write during the exit interview. Headhunters tell candidates that their resignation letters should be short, uninformative, and unequivocal, as in the following example:

> Dear (Employer):
> Please accept this as my official notice of resignation. I appreciate the work we have been able to accomplish together at (Company Name), but I have now made a commitment to another organization, and plan to begin with them in two weeks. Know that it is my intention to work diligently with you to wrap up as much as possible in the next two weeks to make my resignation as smooth as possible. If you have any suggestions on how we can best accomplish that goal, I hope you will share your thoughts with me, as I am eager to leave on the most positive note possible.
> Sincerely,

Scott emphasizes to his candidates that in their exit interviews they should say nothing negative about the firm or their boss and should not explain their resignation:

> [I] tell them, don't say anything negative in your exit interview, nothing, [even though] you're going to want to do it, you're

going to want to get into a pissing contest, you're going to want
to tell the boss he's the biggest horse's behind in the world.
Don't do it. You'll get more satisfaction in walking out of there
saying, "I've really decided just to take a different direction
with my career, thank you for the opportunity you gave me,
I've learned a lot from you, and go on." Because he's going to
know you're lying, and it's going to bug the hell out of him. If
you sit there and conflict with him, it's going to make him
happy. . . . The other thing I'd say to them when they're going
to resign, make it as short and sweet as possible.

[Candidate:] "Well, how can you say that, Scott? I've been
employed here five years."

[Scott:] "Well, Marcy, let me tell you, if they were going to
lay you off or fire you, how would it be? Would they sit there
and talk to you for a half hour? No, they'd make it as short and
sweet as possible. So you owe them the same thing they're
going to owe you."

Scripting a candidate's exit interview—a process other headhunters refer to as "babying" or "coaching"—has advantages additional to that of mitigating the awkwardness associated with this particular interaction. A candidate who won't discuss her reasons for
leaving or provide any information about her new employer is much
more difficult to counteroffer, although that won't necessarily stop
her old boss from trying. From the headhunter's perspective, therefore, a well-managed resignation is one that is short on both information and time, makes the candidate impervious to a counteroffer, and
leads the candidate irresistibly to her new job.

The process of closing the sale confirms how similar headhunters
are to other sales occupations. The ABC of selling ("Always Be Closing") applies as much to headhunters as it does to those selling real
estate or automobiles or insurance. It is also a reminder of the emotional context of getting and receiving a job offer. A client and candidate must like each other, and continue to like each other, for the
engagement expressed in the job offer to culminate in the consum-
mation of its acceptance. Headhunters have to tread carefully over
this emotional terrain and are most effective if they can lower the
heat of the offer-acceptance process by keeping the parties isolated
from each other. It is in being a buffering intermediary that headhunters distinguish themselves not only from other sales personnel,

who deal with only one buyer not two, but also from the intermediaries we discussed at the beginning of this chapter, such as investment bankers and securities analysts, whose job it is to certify the value of the deal, not to isolate the participants.

Headhunters themselves take full advantage of the emotionality of the job offer by manipulating the sentiments of the candidate. They inflate a candidate's sense of uncertainty and anxiety regarding the amount of the offer in order to make it appear better than expected. They magnify the danger of accepting a counteroffer in order to make a candidate too fearful to accept it. They emphasize the risks of a candidate's explaining his departure to his current employer in order to prevent the candidate from contemplating the benefits of not resigning. Headhunters, therefore, close their candidates by controlling their emotions.

Conclusion

In chapter 2 we posed the three central questions of this book. First, how do headhunters persuade employers and job candidates to sell themselves to each other? Second, what do employers gain by using headhunters? Third, what criteria do headhunters use in choosing job candidates? Our answers demonstrate that weak third parties may be able to dominate interactions with stronger parties, that hiring is a social process, and that the hiring decision is a romantic one.

The Power of a Weak Third Party

Our answer to the first question shows how a weak third party manages to control the interaction between itself and two other parties, as well as between these parties themselves, in order to accomplish a sale. The economics of contingency headhunting, we have noted, is highly unfavorable to headhunters: they are paid only if they make the placement, and they seldom enjoy exclusive relationships with clients or long-term relationships with candidates. It is an industry that is easy to enter and that encourages unfettered competition among the firms vying to make placements. Headhunters are entrepreneurs who risk failure (i.e., earning nothing) every time they seek to make a placement. Their clients are not dependent on them, and they rarely have the benefit of embedded ties with clients or candidates to shield them from the rigors of the open market, as has been observed in studies of other entrepreneurs (e.g., Faulkner 1983; Larson 1992; Portes and Sensenbrenner 1993; Uzzi 1997).

The headhunters' predicament can best be appreciated by contrasting their manifest powerlessness to the far more favorable position of service providers in other industries. Consider, for example, the relationship of freelance Hollywood composers with their clients, as portrayed in Faulkner's (1983) study. In this highly competitive business most freelancers work very little, but nearly half of all films are scored by just 10 percent of the composers. Some of these top composers form relatively enduring ties with certain producers and directors, working with them repeatedly. Faulkner argues that the dominance of a highly productive and visible elite of freelance composers, who are closely linked to leading filmmakers, is a direct consequence of the rise of big-budget filmmaking. Producers who have risked enormous sums of money on their projects are reluctant to take additional gambles on unknown composers; consequently, they seek out established, preferably award-winning, composers with proven records of success in an attempt to reduce some of the uncertainty associated with commercial movie making. Faulkner concludes that the existence of this elite challenges the assumption that clients have all the power and shop around to find the cheapest and most pliable service providers. In what he calls a "resource-alternative theory," it is the clients—the filmmakers—who are dependent on the service providers: "There is a countervailing market strength in the inner circle of freelancers because employers with big-budgeted projects need high-profile 'names'" (1983, 235).

Headhunters are not exactly analogous to composers—composers, unlike headhunters, are not third-party brokers—but they are alike in that both provide scarce and valued products to clients. Economic success for headhunters and composers rests on managing their dependence on clients: ensuring that clients choose their products rather than another provider's. Faulkner's analysis suggests that composers enjoy two structural advantages over headhunters in handling clients. The first is the willingness of clients to pay a premium to secure the services of the top composers. The reason is that filmmakers are actually buying the composer's reputation rather than the music, whose quality it is often quite difficult for them to rate. Consequently, they have little or no interest in the products of unheralded composers. Employers, in contrast, though by no means indifferent to a headhunter's reputation, are evaluators and buyers of products, that is, candidates. Their wariness toward a headhunter with whom they have not done business in the past does not prevent them from considering the candidates generated by an unfamiliar source.

The other advantage composers have is that they do not work on a contingency basis. In theory, at least, a filmmaker could request scores from a number of composers for a film and then select the one he or she liked best, but composers, especially established composers, do not write scores without some guarantee of payment. Similarly, a filmmaker could in theory pay all the composers for all the scores that were commissioned, but that would be a very costly way to do business. The result, in practice, is that a filmmaker commissions a single score and does not, therefore, have the opportunity to review multiple scores for his or her film. Headhunting, however, is contingency work, which means there is no cost to an employer (other than the delay in filling the position) in reviewing candidates from more than one headhunter. The consequence for headhunters is that notwithstanding the strong ties that many form with clients, they are unable to convert these ties into bonds of dependence, as composers do with their clients.

The implication of this argument is that since headhunters have neither the power to compel clients to use their services nor the personal connections that could help them achieve the same result, they must rely on their ability to manage market relations. Successful headhunting means having the persistence to make cold call after cold call in search of a viable job order or a likely candidate, the judgment to decide which job orders and potential candidates warrant attention and which are likely to prove fruitless, and finally, the patience to overcome whatever obstacles might lie in the path of a match between client and candidate.

Despite their disadvantages, headhunters are not mere atomized agents bobbing helplessly in the sea of economic exchange. They cope with risk in four ways. First, headhunters pursue long-term relationships with clients in which, ideally, they are assigned repeat business on an exclusive basis. These relationships present the risk, though, that headhunters will become dependent on one or two key clients and will be vulnerable should that business be lost. Second, headhunters are suspicious of clients. They assume clients are actually or probably untrustworthy because they are believed to be willing to accept candidates from headhunters with whom they have no prior relationship. The wariness with which they regard clients prepares headhunters for the possibility that they could lose the placement to an unknown headhunter. It also legitimizes their decision to violate one of the unwritten rules of headhunting by recruiting a candidate from a client, thereby turning that client into a source. Third, headhunters actively create job candidates and do not passively wait for them to materialize. This process involves identifying qualified candidates and then recruiting them. Headhunters turn employees into candidates by illuminating and then aggravating any sources of discontent an employee might reveal. Fourth, headhunters direct and shape the impressions that clients and candidates form of each other before, during, and after the job interview. By positioning themselves between client and candidate, headhunters control the information each side receives and, therefore, the perceptions each forms of the other. Headhunters succeed by first bridging the gap between client and candidate and then buffering each from the other.

The case of headhunting discloses some limitations of both Granovetter's embeddedness approach and Burt's structural-hole approach to economic transactions. Granovetter, for example, has suggested that headhunters are likely to be based on occupational networks: "Though there have been no systematic studies of 'headhunters' who provide prospective employees to corporations, it is common to hear that such companies were formed by people previously in a particular industry whose success depends on their former occupational networks" (1995, 167). Burt has argued that entrepreneurs, such as headhunters, who fill structural holes avoid transactions in which they are providing the same product as other entrepreneurs and are unable to prevent themselves from being pitted against one another, a condition he terms *redundancy* (1992, 38–45). Headhunters, however, survive and flourish without being networked to clients (or candidates) and without being able to curb competition among themselves. They are effective, despite being weak agents, because they have learned how to manage and manipulate their more powerful principals. Their influence rests on their ability to sell their products: jobs and people. Our study supports Wayne Baker's observation that organizations, through the direct management of market ties, can reduce dependence and solve principal-agent problems "even if they do not embed market exchange in social relations or engage in the use of other nonmarket tactics" (1990, 619).

A corollary conclusion is that headhunting demonstrates that trust may be a less consistent feature of economic exchanges than is often assumed. Much of the literature on networks identifies trust as the glue that binds the relationship between buyer and supplier (Dore 1983), manufacturer and subcontractor (Uzzi 1997), and entrepreneur and partner (Larson 1992). These studies suggest that evidence of high levels of trust can be seen in the expectations that both parties should be honest and frank with one another, that they should not act in a self-interested or opportunistic way at the other's expense, and that each party should be willing to perform favors and provide special treatment for the other without reliance on formal reciprocation. Bradach and Eccles (1989), in fact, argue that trust should be considered a third type of control mechanism alongside price and authority, which are associated with markets and hierarchies, respectively.

Headhunters' relations with their clients, in contrast, are far more adversarial. They are similar to those between investment bankers and their corporate clients, which, according to Eccles and Crane, are characterized by "a lack of trust" (1988, 69). Eccles and Crane argue that mistrust originated in the shift from single-bank to multiple-bank relationships: most corporations and other issuers of securities now use more than one investment bank when doing deals. This change, which was designed to capitalize on the growth and increased volatility of the securities market, has led customers and bankers to complain that their dealings with each other have become much more "transactional." Their complaints are strikingly similar to what we have observed in headhunter-client relationships. Bankers criticize customers for treating them as substitutable; they are unhappy when customers with whom they believe they have a relationship use other bankers. For their part, customers distrust their bankers; they fear that these bankers may be tempted to use their knowledge of customers in the service of an acquiring company at some future date, the investment-banking equivalent of a headhunter raiding a client company for candidates.

The conflict and mistrust in headhunter-client and banker-client relationships reflect the fact that in each relationship there is a strong economic incentive for clients to have multiple providers. Competition among providers—especially, in the case of headhunters, hidden competition—produces the most desirable outcomes for clients. It means, however, that headhunters have little faith in clients and place little stock in loyalty toward them.

The other party with whom headhunters must deal are candidates. Candidates are customers, in the sense that they must be persuaded to "buy" the product the headhunter is offering, but they are not fee payers. This fact makes the candidate-headhunter relationship far looser and more informal than the client-headhunter relationship. Headhunters' behavior toward candidates is similar to that of other salesworkers whose livelihood depends on turning prospects into customers (e.g., Leidner 1993; Oakes 1990; Prus 1989a). What makes headhunters different from sellers of life insurance or automobiles, however, is that the product is another person (the hiring manager) and this person is himself a buyer (of job candidates). Headhunters cope with the intricacies and pitfalls of the double sale by using a complex strategy that ranges from impression management to isolating the parties, thereby demonstrating that third parties derive their influence as much from keeping the parties apart as they do from linking them.

Hiring Is a Social Process

Our answer to the question regarding what employers gain by using headhunters demonstrates that hiring is a social process as well as an economic one. There is little doubt that headhunters are very effective in identifying good candidates quickly, especially those who are not active job seekers. It is quite rational and efficient for an employer that wants to find the top candidates for a position without delay to entrust the search to a headhunter. But headhunters' value to their clients also lies in the buffer they provide between the hiring manager and HR, the protection they offer against allegations of employee poaching from rivals and customers, and the psychological mastery of prospects that enables them to turn potential candidates into job seekers and, subsequently, job takers.

The implication of this answer is that economic decisions—in this case, an employer's assigning the search for new employees to a third party—may require explanations that combine market-efficiency arguments (such as Williamson's transaction-costs approach) with organizational-politics arguments. Organizations are political arenas because they are peopled by actors with different and often conflicting interests or "worldviews," to use Robert Thomas's (1994) term. It has long been recognized, for example, that the various functional departments within organizations, such as production and sales, often have competing goals and that organizational outcomes depend on which group has the upper hand (Crozier 1964; Pondy 1967; Thompson 1967; Walton and Dutton 1969).

Baker's (1990) examination of the relationships between corporations and investment banks provides powerful evidence of the compatibility of efficiency and power explanations. He shows that corporate finance managers (CFMs) have intentionally shifted from using a single investment bank as a source of capital to using multiple banks in order to reduce their dependence on these banks and to encourage competition among them. He concludes: "Corporations directly manipulate the number and intensity of market ties to pursue the objectives of independence, uncertainty reduction, and efficiency. . . . The efficiency benefits of competition are obtained because power and efficiency motives are compatible, jointly driving CFMs in the same direction" (1990, 618–620). A similar combination of factors explains why organizations have candidate search performed by outside agents rather than by members of the organization: the externalization decision reflects the power of hiring managers, strengthens their position at the expense of HR, and generates good job candidates.

The role of headhunters is unlikely to diminish even with the emergence of Web sites dedicated to matching jobs and job seekers, such as Monster.com, Hotjobs.com, and Headhunter.net. These sites, which enable employers to post job openings and candidates to post résumés, are an online version of newspaper advertisements. Internet job boards have a number of advantages over their print counterparts. They increase the speed and reduce the cost of job search: a job candidate can immediately send his or her résumé to an employer with a mouse click and avoid the time and expense of stationery and stamps. Candidates are also able to search listings by industry, occupation, and location. For employers, it has been estimated that the cost of placing an ad on a job board is about 5 percent of that of listing a help-wanted ad in a newspaper for thirty days, with the additional benefit of being able to reach candidates all over the country (*New York Times*, July 20, 2000).

"E-cruiting" is, however, a bigger threat to the classified sections of newspapers than to headhunters. At best, it is still a want-ad and résumé service, which means that a job seeker cannot tell what a job or employer is really like and an employer cannot tell if a candidate has the right chemistry. Further, readers of Internet job boards are likely to be the same as those who read newspaper ads: the unemployed and the unhappy. If employers want to find and hire employees who are not looking to change jobs, if they want to conduct their searches in secret, or if they want to poach employees from their rivals, they will continue to use headhunters. For potential candidates who have jobs, talking to a headhunter still carries far less risk of being considered disloyal to one's employer than submitting a résumé electronically. Job boards actually help headhunters identify which employers are looking for candidates and where to find prospects to add to their databases. But the actual match of employer and candidate remains a social process and, therefore, continues to be a relationship that headhunters seek to create and control.

The Romance of the Hiring Decision

Our answer to the third question (the criteria headhunters use in choosing job candidates) attests to the emotional and even romantic side of the hiring decision. In selecting candidates, headhunters look first for an ability to do the job. Once this criterion has been met, however, headhunters choose candidates who will fit in well with clients and, most important, will be liked by hiring managers. A point that headhunters continually emphasized to us was how much hiring depended on the strength of the mutual attraction that developed between client and candidate. Consequently, a headhunter looks for candidates who have the appearance, attitudes, interests, and background that will appeal to the hiring manager, factors that are key, headhunters believe, to generating the chemistry that will produce the job offer. Having located likely prospects and persuaded them to make themselves available as candidates, headhunters prep them to ensure that they actually emphasize their chemistry-generating characteristics during the interview. Clients are also prepped to make certain they do not overlook these points of compatibility. Headhunters thus not only recruit candidates who they believe will like and be liked by their clients but also actively work on getting each party to recognize how likable the other is.

The implication of this finding is that organizational scholars such as Jackall (1988) and Kanter (1993) have underestimated the role of chemistry in hiring decisions. They argue that chemistry is the primary consideration when an employee or candidate's performance is difficult to evaluate—which is a characteristic of senior managerial positions. Our research, however, shows that chemistry is preeminent in every headhunter-conducted search, which includes a far wider range of jobs than just those in senior management. If chemistry is indeed as important a factor in search and hiring decisions as our evidence indicates, it comes at a price: when employers hire people they like, diversity in the workplace is discouraged. A considerable body of psychological evidence has found that people like (and trust) those who are socially similar to themselves, which means headhunters, in an effort to find the most likable candidates, look for and present those who are socially similar to hiring managers.

Headhunters' use of chemistry as a search criterion undoubtedly contributes to the continuation of discrimination in the workplace, for several reasons. One is the simple place-or-perish logic of contingency search: if clients tend to favor candidates who are socially similar to them, it is folly for any headhunter to present candidates who are dissimilar to them. The second is that a headhunter may infer a taste for discrimination on the part of a client, based on the client's past hiring decisions, even in cases in which such an assumption is unwarranted. The third is that a client may indeed have clear, if unstated, preferences for candidates who meet certain ascriptive criteria. In this regard it is worth reiterating that age and appearance play a more prominent role in headhunters' searches than race or gender. Headhunters were more likely to say that their clients wanted candidates who were young and attractive than that they wanted someone of a particular race or gender (diversity searches excluded). Of course, appearance can also be a proxy for these other variables: a search in which the ideal candidate is tall and athletic and has a commanding presence will undoubtedly result in more men being identified than women.

Finally, we predict that the emergence of the "new economy" is likely to magnify the importance of chemistry and, therefore, the lack of diversity. Technology startup companies have intentionally rejected the hierarchy of positions and clearly defined job descriptions of old-economy organizations in favor of fluid, decentralized structures without clear lines of authority or fixed job duties. Employees are expected to be versatile, creative, and willing to spend long hours on the job, although not necessarily always at work in the traditional sense—these firms have, for example, brought game rooms into the workplace to give their employees the opportunity to play while at work (Gladwell 2000). As Malcolm Gladwell has observed, in an environment "where the workplace doubles as the rec room, the particulars of your personality matter a great deal" (2000, 86). Where work and play are combined, it becomes even more probable that hiring managers will prefer those candidates with whom they seem likely to get along and who have similar recreational interests.

References

Althauser, Robert P., and Arne L. Kalleberg. 1981. "Firms, Occupations, and the Structure of Labor Markets: A Conceptual Analysis." In *Sociological Perspectives on Labor Markets*, edited by Ivar Berg, pp. 119–149. New York: Academic Press.

Baker, Wayne E. 1990. "Market Networks and Corporate Behavior." *American Journal of Sociology* 96:589–625.

Baker, Wayne E., and Robert R. Faulkner. 1991a. "Role as Resource in the Hollywood Film Industry." *American Journal of Sociology* 97:279–309.

——. 1991b. "Strategies for Managing Suppliers of Professional Services." *California Management Review* 33:33–45.

Baron, Robert A. 1989. "Impression Management by Applicants During the Employment Interview: The 'Too Much of a Good Thing' Effect." In *The Employment Interview: Theory, Research, and Practice*, edited by Robert W. Eder and Gerald R. Ferris, pp. 204–215. Newbury Park, Calif.: Sage.

Baron, James N., and Jeffrey Pfeffer. 1994. "The Social Psychology of Organizations and Inequality." *Social Psychology Quarterly* 57:190–209.

Baumeister, Roy F. 1982. "A Self-Presentational View of Social Phenomena." *Psychological Bulletin* 91:3–26.

Benson, Susan Porter. 1988. *Counter Cultures: Saleswomen, Managers, and Customers in American Department Stores, 1890–1940*. Urbana: University of Illinois Press.

Bielby, William T., and Denise D. Bielby. 1999. "Organizational Mediation of Project-Based Labor Markets: Talent Agencies and the Careers of Screenwriters." *American Sociological Review* 64:64–85.

Biggart, Nicole Woolsey. 1989. *Charismatic Capitalism: Direct Selling Organizations in America*. Chicago: University of Chicago Press.

Bills, David B. 1988. "Educational Credentials and Promotions: Does Schooling Do More Than Get You in the Door?" *Sociology of Education* 61:52–60.

Bradach, Jeffrey L., and Robert G. Eccles. 1989. "Markets versus Hierarchies: From Ideal Types to Plural Forms." *Annual Review of Sociology* 15:97–118.

Bretz, Robert D., Sara L. Rynes, and Barry Gerhart. 1993. "Recruiter Perceptions of Applicant Fit: Implications for Individual Career Preparation and Job Search Behavior." *Journal of Vocational Behavior* 43:310–327.

Burt, Ronald S. 1992. *Structural Holes: The Social Structure of Competition*. Cambridge: Harvard University Press.

———. 1997. "The Contingent Value of Social Capital." *Administrative Science Quarterly* 42:339–365.

Cardy, Robert L., and Gregory H. Dobbins. 1986. "Affect and Appraisal Accuracy: Liking as an Integral Dimension in Evaluating Performance." *Journal of Applied Psychology* 71:672–678.

Chatman, Jennifer A. 1991. "Matching People and Organizations: Selection and Socialization in Public Accounting Firms." *Administrative Science Quarterly* 36:459–484.

Christopher, Susan, and Michael Storper. 1989. "The Effects of Flexible Specialization on Industrial Politics and the Labor Market: The Motion Picture Industry." *Industrial and Labor Relations Review* 42:331–347.

Ciulla, Joanne B. 2000. *The Working Life: The Promise and Betrayal of Modern Work*. New York: Random House.

Cole, Kenneth J. 1985. *The Headhunter Strategy: How to Make It Work for You*. New York: Wiley.

Collins, Sharon M. 1997. *Black Corporate Executives: The Making and Breaking of a Black Middle Class*. Philadelphia: Temple University Press.

Cook, Karen S., and Richard M. Emerson. 1984. "Exchange Networks and the Analysis of Complex Organizations." *Research in the Sociology of Organizations* 3:1–30.

Crozier, Michel. 1964. *The Bureaucratic Phenomenon*. Chicago: University of Chicago Press.

Dipboye, Robert L., and Barbara B. Gaugler. 1993. "Cognitive and Behavioral Processes in the Selection Interview." In *Personnel Selection in Organizations*, edited by Neal Schmitt and Walter C. Borman, pp. 135–170. San Francisco: Jossey-Bass.

Doeringer, Peter B., and Michael J. Piore. 1971. *Internal Labor Markets and Manpower Analysis*. Lexington, Mass.: Heath.

Dore, Ronald. 1983. "Goodwill and the Spirit of Market Capitalism." *British Journal of Sociology* 34:459–482.

Dorsey, David. 1994. *The Force*. New York: Random House.

Eccles, Robert G., and Dwight B. Crane. 1988. *Doing Deals: Investment Banks at Work*. Boston: Harvard Business School Press.

Eccles, Robert G., and Harrison C. White. 1988. "Price and Authority in

Inter-Profit Center Transactions." In *Organizations and Institutions: Sociological and Economic Approaches to the Analysis of Social Structure*, edited by Christopher Winship and Sherwin Rosen, pp. S17–S51. Supplement to the *American Journal of Sociology* 94.

Emerson, Richard M. 1962. "Power-Dependence Relations." *American Sociological Review* 27:31–41.

Faulkner, Robert R. 1983. *Music on Demand: Composers and Careers in the Hollywood Film Industry*. New Brunswick, N.J.: Transaction Books.

Faulkner, Robert R., and Andy B. Anderson. 1987. "Short-Term Projects and Emergent Careers: Evidence from Hollywood." *American Journal of Sociology* 92:879–909.

Ferris, Gerald R., Thomas R. King, Timothy A. Judge, and K. Michelle Kacmar. 1991. "The Management of Shared Meaning in Organizations: Opportunism in the Reflection of Attitudes, Beliefs, and Values." In *Applied Impression Management: How Image-Making Affects Managerial Decisions*, edited by Robert A. Giacalone and Robert A. Rosenfeld, pp. 41–64. Newbury Park, Calif.: Sage.

Fletcher, Clive. 1989. "Impression Management in the Selection Interview." In *Impression Management in the Organization*, edited by Robert A. Giacalone and Paul Rosenfeld, pp. 269–281. Hillsdale, N.J.: Lawrence Erlbaum Associates.

Fligstein, Neil. 1985. "The Spread of the Multidivisional Form among Large Firms, 1919–1979." *American Sociological Review* 50:377–391.

Frenkel, Stephen J., Marek Korczynski, Karen A. Shire, and May Tam. 1999. *On the Front Line: Organization of Work in the Information Economy*. Ithaca: Cornell University Press.

Geertz, Clifford. 1978. "The Bazaar Economy: Information and Search in Peasant Marketing." *American Economic Review* 68:28–32.

Giacalone, Robert A. 1985. "On Slipping When You Thought You Had Put Your Best Foot Forward: Self-Promotion, Self-Destruction, and Entitlements." *Group and Organization Studies* 10:61–80.

Giacalone, Robert A., and Paul Rosenfeld (eds.). 1989. *Impression Management in the Organization*. Hillsdale, N.J.: Lawrence Erlbaum Associates.

Gilmore, David C., and Gerald R. Ferris. 1989. "The Politics of the Employment Interview." In *The Employment Interview: Theory, Research, and Practice*, edited by Robert W. Eder and Gerald R. Ferris, pp. 195–203. Newbury Park, Calif.: Sage.

Gladwell, Malcolm. 2000. "The New-Boy Network: What Do Job Interviews Really Tell Us?" *New Yorker*, May 29.

Goffman, Erving. 1959. *The Presentation of Self in Everyday Life*. Garden City, N.Y.: Doubleday.

Goodwin, Marjorie Harness. 1990. *He-Said-She-Said: Talk as Social Organization among Black Children*. Bloomington: Indiana University Press.

Granovetter, Mark. 1985. "Economic Action and Social Structure: The Problem of Embeddedness." *American Journal of Sociology* 91:481–510.

———. 1988. "The Sociological and Economic Approaches to Labor Markets Analysis: A Social Structural Approach." In *Industries, Firms, and Jobs: Sociological and Economic Approaches*, edited by George Farkas and Paula England, pp. 187–216. New York: Plenum.

———. 1995. *Getting a Job: A Study of Contacts and Careers*. 2d ed. Chicago: University of Chicago Press.

Hallwood, C. Paul. 1990. *Transaction Costs and Trade between Multinational Corporations*. Boston: Unwin Hyman.

Harrison, Bennett. 1994. *Lean and Mean: The Changing Landscape of Corporate Power in an Age of Flexibility*. New York: Basic Books.

Hatch, Julie, and Angela Clinton. 2000. "Job Growth in the 1990s: A Retrospect." *Monthly Labor Review* (December): 3–18.

Hochschild, Arlie Russell. 1983. *The Managed Heart: Commercialization of Human Feeling*. Berkeley: University of California Press.

Isen, Alice M. 1987. "Positive Affect, Cognitive Processes, and Social Behavior." *Advances in Experimental Social Psychology* 20:203–253.

Jackall, Robert. 1988. *Moral Mazes: The World of Corporate Managers*. New York: Oxford University Press.

Jacobs, Jerry A. (ed.). 1995. *Gender Inequality at Work*. Thousand Oaks, Calif.: Sage.

Jacoby, Sanford M. 1997. *Modern Manors: Welfare Capitalism since the New Deal*. Princeton: Princeton University Press.

Kacmar, K. Michelle, John E. Delery, and Gerald R. Ferris. 1992. "Differential Effectiveness of Applicant Impression Management Tactics on Employment Interview Decisions." *Journal of Applied Social Psychology* 22:1250–1272.

Kalleberg, Arne L., David Knoke, Peter V. Marsden, and Joe L. Spaeth. 1996. *Organizations in America: Analyzing Their Structures and Human Resource Practices*. Thousand Oaks, Calif.: Sage.

Kane, Emily W., and Laura J. Macaulay. 1993. "Interviewer Gender and Gender Attitudes." *Public Opinion Quarterly* 57:1–28.

Kanter, Rosabeth Moss. 1993. *Men and Women of the Corporation*. 2d ed. New York: Basic Books.

Keenan, A. 1977. "Some Relationships between Interviewers' Personal Feelings about Candidates and Their General Evaluation of Them." *Journal of Occupational Psychology* 50:275–283.

Kennelly, Ivy. 1999. "'That Single-Mother Element': How White Employers Typify Black Women." *Gender and Society* 13:168–192.

Kramer, Roderick M., Marilynn B. Brewer, and Benjamin A. Hanna. 1996. "Collective Trust and Collective Action." In *Trust in Organizations: Frontiers of Theory and Research*, edited by Roderick M. Kramer and Tom R. Tyler, pp. 357–389. Thousand Oaks, Calif.: Sage.

Larson, Andrea. 1992. "Network Dyads in Entrepreneurial Settings: A Study of the Governance of Exchange Relationships." *Administrative Science Quarterly* 37:76–104.

Lazerson, Mark H. 1988. "Organizational Growth of Small Firms: An Outcome of Markets and Hierarchies?" *American Sociological Review* 53:330–342.

Leidner, Robin. 1993. *Fast Food, Fast Talk: Service Work and the Routinization of Everyday Life*. Berkeley: University of California Press.

Levinthal, Daniel A., and Mark Fichman. 1988. "Dynamics of Interorganizational Attachments: Auditor-Client Relationships." *Administrative Science Quarterly* 33:345–369.

Liden, Robert C., and Charles K. Parsons. 1989. "Understanding Interpersonal Behavior in the Employment Interview: A Reciprocal Interactional Analysis." In *The Employment Interview: Theory, Research, and Practice*, edited by Robert W. Eder and Gerald R. Ferris, pp. 219–232. Newbury Park, Calif.: Sage.

Lin, Thung-Rung, Gregory H. Dobbins, and Jiing-Lih Farh. 1992. "A Field Study of Race and Age Similarity Effects on Interviewer Ratings in Conventional and Situational Interviews." *Journal of Applied Psychology* 77:363–371.

Lucht, John. 1988. *Rites of Passage at $100,000+: The Insider's Guide to Absolutely Everything about Executive Job-Changing*. New York: Viceroy.

Malone, Thomas W., and Robert J. Laubacher. 1998. "The Dawn of the E-Lance Economy." *Harvard Business Review* 76 (September–October): 145–152.

Manser, Marilyn E., and Garnett Picot. 1999. "The Role of Self-Employment in U.S. and Canadian Job Growth." *Monthly Labor Review* 122 (April): 10–25.

Martinez, Tomas. 1976. *The Human Marketplace: An Examination of Private Employment Agencies*. New Brunswick, N.J.: Transaction Books.

Mayfield, Eugene C., and Robert E. Carlson. 1966. "Selection Interview Decisions: First Results from a Long-Term Research Project." *Personnel Psychology* 19:41–53.

McCammon, Holly J., and Larry J. Griffin. 2000. "Workers and Their Customers and Clients: An Editorial Introduction." *Work and Occupations* 27:278–293.

Monthly Labor Review Online. 2000. "Employee Tenure in 2000." 123, 9 (September). Internet address: http://stats.bls.gov/newsrels.htm.

Moore, Wilbert. 1962. *The Conduct of the Corporation*. New York: Random House Vintage.

Morrill, Calvin. 1995. *The Executive Way: Conflict Management in Corporations*. Chicago: University of Chicago Press.

Oakes, Guy. 1990. *The Soul of the Salesman: The Moral Ethos of Personal Sales*. Atlantic Highlands, N.J.: Humanities Press International.

Osterman, Paul. 1999. *Securing Prosperity: The American Labor Market: How It Has Changed and What to Do about It*. Princeton: Princeton University Press.

Partnoy, Frank. 1997. *F.I.A.S.C.O.: The Inside Story of a Wall Street Trader*. New York: Penguin Books.

Perrow, Charles. 1986. *Complex Organizations: A Critical Essay*. New York: Random House.

Pfeffer, Jeffrey. 1987. "A Resource Dependence Perspective on Intercorporate Relations." In *Intercorporate Relations: The Structural Analysis of Business*, edited by Mark S. Mizruchi and Michael Schwartz, pp. 25–55. Cambridge: Cambridge University Press.

———. 1989. "A Political Perspective on Careers: Interests, Networks, and Environments." In *Handbook of Career Theory*, edited by Michael B. Arthur, Douglas T. Hall, and Barbara S. Lawrence, pp. 380–396. New York: Cambridge University Press.

Pierce, Jennifer L. 1995. *Gender Trials: Emotional Lives in Contemporary Law Firms*. Berkeley: University of California Press.

Pink, Daniel H. 1997. "Free Agent Nation." *Fast Company* 12 (December). Internet address:
http://www.fastcompany.com/online/12/freeagent.html.

Pondy, Louis R. 1967. "Organizational Conflict: Concepts and Models." *Administrative Science Quarterly* 17:296–320.

Portes, Alejandro, and Julia Sensenbrenner. 1993. "Embeddedness and Immigration: Notes on the Social Determinants of Economic Action." *American Journal of Sociology* 98:1320–1350.

Powell, Walter W. 1985. *Getting into Print: The Decision-Making Process in Scholarly Publishing*. Chicago: University of Chicago Press.

———. 1990. "Neither Market nor Hierarchy: Network Forms of Organization." *Research in Organizational Behavior* 12:295–336.

Prus, Robert C. 1989a. *Pursuing Customers: An Ethnography of Marketing Activities*. Newbury Park, Calif.: Sage.

———. 1989b. *Making Sales: Influence as Interpersonal Accomplishment.* Newbury Park, Calif.: Sage.

Rand, Thomas M., and Kenneth N. Wexley. 1975. "Demonstration of the Effect, 'Similar to Me,' in Simulated Employment Interviews." *Psychological Reports* 36:535–544.

Reich, Robert B. 1991. *The Work of Nations: Preparing Ourselves for Twenty-first-Century Capitalism.* New York: Vintage Books.

Reskin, Barbara, and Debra Branch McBrier. 2000. "Why Not Ascription? Organizations' Employment of Male and Female Managers." *American Sociological Review* 65:210–233.

Reskin, Barbara, Debra B. McBrier, and Julie A. Kmec. 1999. "The Determinants and Consequences of Workplace Sex and Race Composition." *Annual Review of Sociology* 25:335–361.

Reskin, Barbara, and Irene Padavic. 1994. *Women and Men at Work.* Thousand Oaks, Calif.: Pine Forge Press.

Rosenfeld, Paul, Robert A. Giacalone, and Catherine A. Riordan. 1995. *Impression Management in Organizations: Theory, Measurement, Practice.* London: Routledge.

Rynes, Sara, and Barry Gerhart. 1990. "Interviewer Assessments of Applicant 'Fit': An Exploratory Investigation." *Personnel Psychology* 43:13–35.

Sackett, Paul R., Laura R. Burris, and Ann Marie Ryan. 1989. "Coaching and Practice Effects in Personnel Selection." In *International Review of Industrial and Organizational Psychology*, edited by Cary L. Cooper and Ivan T. Robertson, pp. 145–183. New York: Wiley.

Seabright, Mark A., Daniel A. Levinthal, and Mark Fichman. 1992. "Role of Individual Attachments in the Dissolution of Interorganizational Relationships." *Academy of Management Journal* 35:122–160.

Seidel, Marc-David L., Jeffrey T. Polzer, and Katherine J. Stewart. 2000. "Friends in High Places: The Effects of Social Networks on Discrimination in Salary Negotiations." *Administrative Science Quarterly* 45:1–24.

Simmel, Georg. 1950. *The Sociology of Georg Simmel.* New York: Free Press.

Smitka, Michael J. 1991. *Competitive Ties: Subcontracting in the Japanese Automotive Industry.* New York: Columbia University Press.

Sokoloff, Natalie J. 1980. *Between Money and Love: The Dialectics of Women's Home and Market Work.* New York: Praeger.

Stinchcombe, Arthur L. 1983. *Economic Sociology.* New York: Academic Press.

Stross, Randall E. 2000. *eBoys: The First Inside Account of Venture Capitalists at Work.* New York: Crown Business.

Thomas, Robert J. 1994. *What Machines Can't Do: Politics and Technol-*

ogy in the Industrial Enterprise. Berkeley: University of California Press.

Thompson, James D. 1967. *Organizations in Action.* New York: McGraw-Hill.

Thurow, Lester. 1975. *Generating Inequality.* New York: Basic Books.

Tilly, Chris, and Charles Tilly. 1998. *Work under Capitalism.* Boulder: Westview Press.

Uzzi, Brian. 1996. "The Sources and Consequences of Embeddedness for the Economic Performance of Organizations: The Network Effect." *American Sociological Review* 61:674–698.

———. 1997. "Social Structure and Competition in Interfirm Networks: The Paradox of Embeddedness." *Administrative Science Quarterly* 42:35–67.

———. 1999. "Embeddedness in the Making of Financial Capital: How Social Relations and Networks Benefit Firms Seeking Financing." *American Sociological Review* 64:481–505.

Walton, Richard E., and John M. Dutton. 1969. "The Management of Interdepartmental Conflict: A Model and a Review." *Administrative Science Quarterly* 14:73–84.

Weitz, Barton A., Stephen B. Castleberry, and John F. Tanner. 1995. *Selling: Building Partnerships.* Chicago: Irwin.

White, Harrison C. 1992. "Agency as Control in Formal Networks." In *Networks and Organizations: Structure, Form, and Action,* edited by Nitin Nohria and Robert G. Eccles, pp. 92–117. Boston: Harvard Business School Press.

Whyte, William H. 1956. *The Organization Man.* New York: Simon and Schuster.

Williamson, Oliver E. 1975. *Markets and Hierarchies: Analysis and Antitrust Implications.* New York: Free Press.

———. 1985. *The Economic Institutions of Capitalism.* New York: Free Press.

———. 1994. "Transaction Cost Economics and Organization Theory." In *The Handbook of Economic Sociology,* edited by Neil J. Smelser and Richard Swedberg, pp. 77–107. Princeton: Princeton University Press and Russell Sage Foundation.

Wilson, Sloan. 1955. *The Man in the Gray Flannel Suit.* New York: Simon and Schuster.

Zuckerman, Ezra W. 1999. "The Categorical Imperative: Securities Analysts and the Illegitimacy Discount." *American Journal of Sociology* 104:1398–1438.

Index